The KitchenAid COOK-BOOK

The

KitchenAid

COOK-BOOK

Published and distributed by Hopkinson & Blake, New York

Copyright © Hobart Corporation, 1983

Hopkinson & Blake, Publishers
1001 Avenue of the Americas
New York, NY 10018

Manufactured in the United States of America

Library of Congress Cataloging in Publication Data
Main entry under title:
The KitchenAid cookbook.
Prepared by the KitchenAid Division, Hobart Corporation.
1. Mixers (Cookery)   I. Hobart Corporation. KitchenAid Division.
TX840.M5K57   1983   641.5'89   83-10747
ISBN 0-911974-30-X

KitchenAid® is a registered trademark of Hobart Corporation.

For David A. Meeker,
whose energy and talents guided
the development of KitchenAid®
home products for over 50 years.

Acknowledgments

For their cheerful and dependable assistance, we extend our deep appreciation to:

Liza Kirby of Ketchum Public Relations, and Valerie Peltzman, who did the initial research and recipe development, as well as the food styling;

Nancy Keske, KitchenAid Home Economist, who tested and rechecked every recipe, and then some, with her usual efficiency;

Shirley Kiser, KitchenAid Publicity Assistant, who tirelessly typed and retyped every word of the manuscript;

Gus Francisco and Allan Baillie, for bringing our recipes to life in their photographs, and Michael Pruzan, for the lovely cover shot;

And Dansk International Designs, for graciously lending us many of the props used for photography.

INTRODUCTION

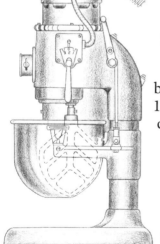

The first KitchenAid mixer, 1919.

The history of KitchenAid goes back to the early years of this century, when Hobart Corporation, as it is known today, was fast becoming a world leader in the manufacturing of equipment for restaurants and bakeries. One of Hobart's first products, introduced in 1915, was a large commercial mixer. It was greeted by chefs and bakers with such enthusiasm that the company began thinking of a smaller version for home use. A household mixer with a full complement of food preparation attachments was marketed for the first time in 1919, bearing the name KitchenAid.

Now that you own a KitchenAid mixer, you will surely be tempted to expand your cooking repertoire. And why not? The versatility of the mixer gives you endless opportunities to grace your table with appealing new dishes that may have been too difficult or time-consuming before.

The purpose of this book is to encourage you to use your mixer to its full advantage. The recipes, from appetizers to desserts, cover every aspect of informal and formal dining. But what's especially important is that they have been developed to reveal the many benefits of your mixer...and to entice you into new and rewarding cooking techniques.

Whether you are already well-versed in the artistry of good cooking, or a novice with big ambitions, or only a sometimes cook with a busy schedule, you will find in these pages a feast of ideas for every occasion.

Many of the recipes were created specifically for your mixer. The others include some time-honored classics, and some popular dishes with new and sometimes unusual twists. Cooking tips and helpful hints on ingredients are sprinkled throughout the book, and in the last chapter you'll find information on KitchenAid mixer attachments and accessories—each designed to make life in the kitchen a lot easier.

All the recipes were tested with Model K45SS and K5SS mixers and attachments. For best results, we suggest you use the exact piece of equipment called for in each recipe. If you have any questions about any of our recipes or products, please write to us. The address is on page 185.

We hope the KitchenAid Cookbook inspires you to make full use of your KitchenAid mixer and to experience the pleasures it offers you. Don't let your mixer languish on the kitchen counter. Use it. Experiment with it. Enjoy it. And before long, you'll wonder how you ever got along without it.

Liz Walsh
Manager, Consumer Information

CONTENTS

Contents

APPETIZERS

Creating a good first impression

From a simple dip to an elegant salmon mousse, appetizers can be the focal point of a cocktail party, the prelude to an elegant dinner, or special lead-in to an otherwise uncomplicated meal. Whatever the occasion, welcome your guests with any one of 20 carefully chosen recipes. Among them, a simple but provocative spread of Roquefort cheese and walnuts; bite-sized appetizer puffs encasing an interesting selection of fillings; or a delectable recipe for Tiropetas, a Greek specialty of creamy feta cheese wrapped with layers of flaky phyllo dough.

Savory Cheese Spread

A low-calorie version of Liptauer (Cream Cheese Spread).

1 cup cottage cheese
½ cup butter or
margarine, softened
1 tablespoon paprika
¼ teaspoon garlic salt
1 teaspoon caraway
seed (optional)
½ teaspoon dry mustard
1 teaspoon dried onion
½ cup sour cream
1 tablespoon chives
or parsley

Assemble and attach Fruit/Vegetable Strainer. Turn to Speed 4 and strain cottage cheese. Set aside.

Place butter in bowl. Attach bowl and flat beater. Turn to Speed 4 and beat 1 minute. Stop and scrape bowl. Add strained cottage cheese, paprika, garlic salt, caraway seed, dry mustard, onion, and sour cream. Turn to Speed 4 and beat until smooth, about 30 seconds. Stop and scrape bowl. Turn to Speed 4 and beat for 30 seconds more.

Shape cheese mixture into a mound. Decorate with chives or parsley. Refrigerate 2 hours or until firm. Serve with assorted crackers.

Yield: 2 cups.

Baba Ghanoush

A Middle Eastern specialty of eggplant puree seasoned with sesame seed paste, fresh lemon and cumin. Great for dipping with vegetables or Arab bread.

2 medium eggplants
¼ cup fresh lemon juice
⅓ cup tahini (sesame
seed paste)
3 cloves garlic, minced
¼ teaspoon salt
½ teaspoon cumin

Prick eggplants with a fork. Place on baking sheet and bake at 400°F for 50 to 60 minutes, or until eggplants collapse and are soft; cool.

Peel and cut open, discarding heavily seeded portions; drain well. Assemble and attach Food Grinder using fine grinding plate. Turn to Speed 4 and grind eggplant into bowl; drain well.

Attach bowl and wire whip. Add remaining ingredients. Turn to Speed 2 and whip 30 seconds. Cover and refrigerate 4 hours to blend flavors.

Yield: 2 cups.

Shrimp Balls
Save these for a crowd you want to impress.

1 pound raw shrimp,
  shelled
⅓ cup water chestnuts
3 slices fresh bread
1 egg, slightly beaten
2 teaspoons minced
  scallions
¼ teaspoon salt
  Oil for deep fat
  frying

Assemble and attach Food Grinder using fine grinding plate. Turn to Speed 4 and grind shrimp, water chestnuts, and bread into bowl. Add egg, scallions, and salt. Attach bowl and flat beater. Turn to Speed 2 and mix 1 minute.

Heat ½-inch oil in heavy skillet to 375°F. Form shrimp mixture into 1-inch balls. Fry in hot oil a few at a time until golden brown. Drain on paper towels. Serve hot with soy sauce and hot Chinese mustard.

Yield: 32 appetizers.

Sausage Stuffed Mushrooms
These bite-size hors d'oeuvres can be prepared ahead of time, heated in the oven as needed, then served piping hot.

30 medium fresh
  mushrooms
1 slice white bread
½ pound pork shoulder
1 tablespoon chopped
  parsley
¾ teaspoon salt
¼ teaspoon sage
⅛ teaspoon pepper
4 ounces mozzarella
  cheese

Remove stems from mushrooms; set caps aside. Assemble and attach Food Grinder with coarse grinding plate. Turn to Speed 4 and grind stems and bread into separate bowls; set aside.

On Speed 4 grind pork into mixer bowl. Add parsley, salt, sage, and pepper. Attach bowl and flat beater. Turn to Speed 2 and mix 1 minute or until well combined. Brown sausage mixture in skillet over medium heat; remove with slotted spoon, leaving fat in pan. Add mushroom stems to fat and saute 3 minutes. Remove from heat and set aside.

Assemble and attach Rotor Slicer/Shredder with fine shredder cone (No. 1). Turn to Speed 4 and shred cheese. In large bowl, combine cheese, mushroom stems, and sausage.

Fill mushroom caps with sausage/cheese mixture. Place on baking sheets and bake at 450°F for 15 minutes. Serve hot.

Yield: 30 appetizers.

Cheese Sticks

Tangy Parmesan cheese and hot red pepper wrapped in flaky puff pastry.

*4 ounces Cheddar
  cheese*
*4 ounces Parmesan
  cheese*
*½ teaspoon red pepper
  flakes*
½ teaspoon oregano
*1 sheet frozen puff
  pastry, defrosted*
1 egg white
1 tablespoon water

Assemble and attach Rotor Slicer/Shredder using fine shredder cone (No. 1). Turn to Speed 4 and shred Cheddar cheese and Parmesan cheese into separate bowls. Add red pepper flakes and oregano to Cheddar cheese and thoroughly combine; set aside.

On lightly floured board, roll pastry to a 15 x 18-inch rectangle. Sprinkle Cheddar cheese mixture over pastry and press lightly into dough. Cut pastry lengthwise into three 5 x 18-inch strips, then horizontally into 1-inch pieces. Twist each piece into a spiral.

Beat egg white and water with fork until foamy. Brush sticks with beaten egg white and roll in Parmesan cheese. Place on greased baking sheets and bake at 425°F for 10 to 12 minutes or until golden. Serve warm.

Yield: 54 appetizers.

Always crumble dried herbs between your fingers just before adding to a recipe. This helps release their full flavor. When fresh herbs are available, remember this general rule of thumb: one tablespoon of freshly chopped herbs equals one teaspoon dried herbs.

Appetizer Puffs
Savory variations on a recurring theme.

1 cup water
½ cup butter or
 margarine
¼ teaspoon salt
1 cup all-purpose flour
4 eggs

Heat water, butter, and salt in a 1½-quart saucepan over high heat to a full rolling boil. Reduce heat and quickly stir in flour, mixing vigorously until mixture leaves sides of pan in a ball.

Place mixture in bowl. Attach bowl and flat beater. Turn to Speed 2 and add eggs, one at a time, beating 30 seconds after each addition. Stop and scrape bowl. Turn to Speed 4 and beat 15 seconds.

Drop dough onto greased cookie sheets forming 30 mounds, 2 inches apart. Bake at 400°F for 10 minutes, then reduce heat to 350°F and bake 25 minutes longer. Cut a small slit in side of each puff. Let stand 10 minutes in turned off oven with door ajar. Cool completely.

Cut off tops and fill with *Sardine and Egg Filling, Crab Dill Filling*, or *Chicken and Pineapple Filling*. Serve immediately.

Yield: 30 appetizers.

Sardine and Egg Filling

1 can (3½ oz.) skinless
 and boneless
 sardines, drained
6 hard cooked eggs
½ small onion
¼ cup mayonnaise
 Salt and pepper

Assemble and attach Food Grinder using coarse grinding plate. Turn to Speed 4 and grind sardines, eggs, and onion into bowl.

Add mayonnaise, salt, and pepper. Attach bowl and flat beater. Turn to Speed 2 and mix 1 minute. Chill mixture thoroughly.

Yield: 2 cups.

Crab Dill Filling

2 cans (6½ oz. each)
 crab meat, drained
2 stalks celery, cut into
 1-inch pieces
½ small onion
1 tablespoon lemon
 juice
¼ teaspoon dill weed
½ cup mayonnaise
 Salt and pepper

Assemble and attach Food Grinder using coarse grinding plate. Turn to Speed 4 and grind crab, celery, and onion into bowl.

Add lemon juice, dill weed, mayonnaise, salt, and pepper. Attach bowl and flat beater. Turn to Speed 2 and mix 1 minute. Chill mixture thoroughly.

Yield: 2 cups.

Chicken and Pineapple Filling

2 cups cooked,
  cubed chicken
2 stalks celery, cut into
  1-inch pieces
1 can (8 oz.) crushed
  pineapple, drained
¼ cup slivered almonds
½ cup mayonnaise
¼ teaspoon paprika
  Salt and pepper

Assemble and attach Food Grinder using coarse grinding plate. Turn to Speed 4 and grind chicken and celery into bowl.

Add pineapple, almonds, mayonnaise, paprika, salt, and pepper. Attach bowl and flat beater. Turn to Speed 2 and mix 1 minute. Chill mixture thoroughly.

Yield: 2 cups.

Texas Bean Dip

4 ounces Monterey Jack
  cheese
1 can (20 oz.) red
  kidney beans
1 cup tomato puree
2 tablespoons chopped
  green chilies
1 teaspoon salt
½ teaspoon ground
  cumin
¼ teaspoon ground
  coriander
1 teaspoon chili
  powder
2 tablespoons butter
  or margarine
½ cup chopped onion
1 clove garlic, minced

Assemble and attach Rotor Slicer/Shredder using fine shredder cone (No. 1). Turn to Speed 4 and shred cheese into bowl. Add beans, tomato puree, chilies, salt, cumin, coriander, and chili powder. Attach bowl and flat beater. Turn to Speed 2 and mix until beans are partially mashed, about 1½ minutes.

Melt butter in large skillet over medium heat. Add onion and garlic and sauté 3 minutes. Add bean mixture and simmer 5 minutes or until cheese melts. Serve warm with taco chips.

Yield: 4 cups.

Salmon Mousse

This delicate recipe belongs in every serious cook's repertoire.

1 tablespoon
   unflavored gelatin
¼ cup cold water
¾ cup mayonnaise
3 tablespoons lemon
   juice
2 stalks celery
1 small onion
1 can (15 oz.) salmon,
   drained
½ teaspoon dried dill
¼ teaspoon salt
⅛ teaspoon pepper
⅓ cup heavy cream

Sprinkle gelatin over ¼ cup cold water in small custard cup; let stand 3 minutes to soften. Bring to boiling 1 inch water in small skillet or saucepan. Set custard cup in water; stir gelatin until dissolved. Add dissolved gelatin to mayonnaise and blend well. Stir in lemon juice.

Assemble and attach Food Grinder using fine grinding plate. Turn to Speed 4 and grind celery, onion, and salmon into a large bowl. Fold in mayonnaise mixture, dill, salt, and pepper.

Place cream in mixer bowl. Attach bowl and wire whip Turn to Speed 10 and whip until stiff. Fold whipped cream into salmon mixture. Spread into lightly oiled 4-cup mold and chill until set, about 2 hours. When ready to serve, unmold and garnish with cucumber slices and watercress.

Yield: 4 cups.

Hot Chili Dip

5 jalapeño chilies
1 large green pepper,
   seeded and cut into
   sixths
5 large tomatoes, peeled
   and cut into sixths
1 small onion, cut into
   sixths
1 clove garlic
½ teaspoon dried
   oregano
1 teaspoon salt

Assemble and attach Food Grinder using coarse grinding plate. Turn to Speed 4 and grind chilies, green pepper, tomatoes, onion, and garlic into bowl. Add oregano and salt. Attach bowl and flat beater. Turn to Speed 2 and mix for 1 minute. Transfer mixture to storage container and refrigerate overnight before serving. Serve with taco chips.

Yield: 4 cups.

Meatball Hors D'Oeuvres

1 pound ground beef
2 egg yolks
⅓ cup dry bread crumbs
⅓ cup Parmesan cheese
2 tablespoons chopped
  parsley
¾ teaspoon garlic salt
½ teaspoon oregano
¼ teaspoon pepper
2 tablespoons chopped
  stuffed olives
¼ cup olive oil
  Tangy Barbecue
  Sauce

Place ground beef, egg yolks, bread crumbs, Parmesan cheese, parsley, garlic salt, oregano, pepper, and olives in bowl. Attach bowl and flat beater. Turn to Speed 2 and mix for 1 minute.

Form mixture into 1-inch balls and fry in olive oil until well browned. Drain on paper towels. Warm *Tangy Barbecue Sauce* and pour over meatballs. Serve warm from chafing dish.

Yield: 30 appetizers.

Tangy Barbecue Sauce

1¼ cups brown sugar
1 cup catsup
1 tablespoon dry
  mustard
2 tablespoons
  Worcestershire sauce
2 tablespoons vinegar
1 cup strong coffee
½ cup finely chopped
  onion
1 teaspoon salt
⅛ teaspoon pepper

Combine all ingredients in a heavy saucepan. Mix well and cook over medium heat 10 minutes, stirring occasionally. Reduce heat and simmer 30 minutes. Cool sauce and store covered in refrigerator until needed.

Yield: 2 cups.

Tiropetas

Bite into layers of flaky phyllo pastry encasing a creamy, melt-in-your-mouth filling.

½ pound feta cheese, drained and crumbled

1 package (3 oz.) cream cheese

½ cup cottage cheese

¼ cup grated Romano cheese

2 eggs

⅛ teaspoon pepper
Dash nutmeg

1 pound frozen prepared phyllo dough, thawed

1 cup butter or margarine, melted

Place feta cheese, cream cheese, and cottage cheese in bowl. Attach bowl and flat beater. Turn to Speed 4 and beat 1 minute, until fluffy. Stop and scrape bowl. Add Romano cheese, pepper, and nutmeg. Turn to Speed 2 and beat 30 seconds. Stop and scrape bowl. Turn to Speed 2 and add eggs, one at a time, beating 30 seconds after each addition. Increase to Speed 4 and beat 15 seconds.

Place 1 sheet phyllo dough on a flat surface. Cover remaining phyllo dough with a slightly damp towel. Brush sheet with butter, top with another sheet and brush again with butter. Cut lengthwise into strips, about 2½ inches wide. Place 1 teaspoon cheese mixture on a bottom corner of strip. Fold over into a traingle shape and continue folding like a flag. Brush with butter and place on greased baking sheet. Repeat with remaining phyllo dough and cheese mixture. Work quickly as phyllo dough dries out quickly. Bake at 350°F for 15 to 20 minutes until golden brown. Serve immediately.

Yield: 48 appetizers.

Swiss and Bacon Canapes

Incredibly easy to prepare—and tasty, too.

¼ pound Swiss cheese

4 slices bacon, crisply cooked and crumbled

⅓ cup evaporated milk

1 teaspoon Worcestershire sauce
Dash pepper

26 bread rounds

Assemble and attach Rotor Slicer/Shredder using fine shredder cone (No. 1). Turn to Speed 4 and shred Swiss cheese into bowl. Add bacon, evaporated milk, Worcestershire sauce, and pepper. Attach bowl and flat beater. Turn to Speed 4 and beat 1 minute. Stop and scrape bowl. Turn to Speed 6 and beat 30 seconds.

Top each bread round with 1 teaspoon of cheese mixture and place on greased baking sheets. Bake at 400°F for 8 to 10 minutes or until lightly browned. Serve immediately.

Yield: 26 appetizers.

Roquefort Nut Spread

½ pound Roquefort
cheese, crumbled

5 tablespoons butter or
margarine, softened

¼ teaspoon cayenne
pepper

1 cup chopped walnuts

Place Roquefort cheese, butter, and cayenne pepper in bowl. Attach bowl and wire whip. Turn to Speed 2 and whip 1 minute. Stop and scrape bowl. Add nuts. Turn to Speed 2 and whip 30 seconds. Serve at room temperature with assorted crackers.

Yield: 1½ cups.

Brewmasters Cheese Spread

Snappy blend of Cheddar and cream cheese, beer and onion.

8 ounces Cheddar
cheese

1 package (8 oz.) cream
cheese, softened

¼ cup beer

½ teaspoon dry mustard

1 teaspoon minced
onion

½ teaspoon Worcester-
shire sauce

Dash cayenne pepper

Assemble and attach Rotor Slicer/Shredder using fine shredder cone (No. 1). Turn to Speed 4 and shred Cheddar cheese into bowl. Add cream cheese, beer, dry mustard, onion, Worcestershire sauce, and cayenne pepper.

Attach bowl and flat beater. Turn to Speed 4 and beat 1 minute. Stop and scrape bowl. Turn to Speed 6 and beat 30 seconds or until fluffy. Serve with assorted crackers.

Yield: 1¾ cups.

Hummus

A well-seasoned puree of chick peas and sesame seed paste.

1 can (20 oz.) chick
  peas, drained
¼ cup cold water
¼ cup fresh lemon juice
¼ cup tahini (sesame
  seed paste)
3 cloves garlic, minced
½ teaspoon salt
¼ teaspoon paprika
  (optional)

Assemble and attach Fruit/Vegetable Strainer. Turn to Speed 4 and strain chick peas into bowl. Return waste to strained chick peas.

Add water, lemon juice, tahini, garlic, salt, and paprika. Attach bowl and wire whip. Turn to Speed 4 and whip 1 minute. Stop and scrape bowl. Increase to Speed 10 and whip 1 minute or until smooth. Serve with toasted Arab bread.

Yield: 2 cups.

Curry Dip

1 cup mayonnaise
½ cup sour cream
1½ teaspoons lemon
  juice
1 teaspoon seasoned
  salt
1 teaspoon chopped
  parsley
1 teaspoon minced
  onion
½ teaspoon Worcester-
  shire sauce
¼ teaspoon salt
¼ teaspoon curry
  powder

Place all ingredients in bowl. Attach bowl and wire whip. Turn to Speed 4 and whip 1 minute. Stop and scrape bowl. Turn to Speed 6 and whip 30 seconds. Chill. Serve with raw vegetables.

Yield: 1½ cups.

Potato Chips

For the perpetual nibbler on a salt-free diet.

2 pounds all-purpose potatoes

1 quart vegetable oil Salt (optional)

Assemble and attach Rotor Slicer/Shredder using thin slicer cone (No. 4). Turn to Speed 4 and slice potatoes.

Cover sliced potatoes in cold water and soak 1 hour. Drain and dry thoroughly.

Heat oil in 5-quart pot over medium heat to 375°F. Fry potatoes in small batches until golden. Drain on paper towels and salt, if desired. Serve immediately.

Yield: 7 cups.

SOUPS

The great soothers

Soup . . . it can be hot and hearty, or cold and refreshing; the subtle beginning to an elegant dinner; or a satisfying meal all by itself. Its tastes and textures are almost unending, as decided by the many fresh ingredients found in your garden, vegetable crisper, or the staples stored in your cupboard. In short, soup is what you make it.

22

French Onion Soup

A culinary classic laced with sherry.

6 medium onions
¼ pound Swiss cheese
⅓ cup butter or margarine
1½ teaspoons sugar
6 cups chicken or beef broth
2 tablespoons dry sherry
8 slices French bread

Assemble and attach Rotor Slicer/Shredder using thick slicer cone (No. 3). Turn to Speed 4 and slice onions; set aside. Exchange thick slicer cone for fine shredder cone (No. 1). Turn to Speed 4 and shred Swiss cheese; set aside.

Melt butter in large pot over medium-high heat. Add onions and sauté 15 minutes until transparent but not browned. Reduce heat and add sugar; continue cooking 20 to 25 minutes. Add broth, cover and simmer 45 minutes. Stir in sherry.

Ladle soup into individual serving bowls. Place one bread slice in each bowl and sprinkle with Swiss cheese. Place under broiler 3 minutes or until cheese melts.

Yield: 8 servings.

Avocado Soup

Smooth introduction to a special dinner.

¼ cup butter or margarine
¼ cup flour
4 cups milk
1 large, very ripe avocado, peeled and pitted
½ teaspoon orange peel
¼ teaspoon ginger

Melt butter in large saucepan over medium heat. Blend in flour and cook until smooth. Gradually stir in milk, keeping mixture smooth. Continue cooking over medium heat until thickened, stirring constantly. Remove from heat and set aside.

Place avocado in bowl. Attach bowl and wire whip. Turn to Speed 6 and mash avocado, about 1 minute. Stop and scrape bowl. Add orange peel and ginger. Turn to Speed 6 and whip 1 minute. Reduce to Stir Speed and slowly add milk mixture, whipping until smooth, about 2 minutes. Refrigerate until well chilled.

Yield: 4 to 6 servings.

Tomato Cheddar Soup

The addition of Cheddar cheese gives this simple but ever-popular soup another dimension.

1 medium onion, quartered

¾ pound Cheddar cheese

¼ cup butter or margarine

¼ cup flour

2 cups chicken broth

2 cups milk

1 can (28 oz.) whole tomatoes, drained, seeded, and chopped

½ teaspoon salt

Assemble and attach Rotor Slicer/Shredder using thin slicer cone (No. 4). Turn to Speed 4 and slice onions; set aside. Exchange thin slicer cone for fine shredder cone (No. 1). Turn to Speed 4 and shred cheese; set aside.

Melt butter in large pot over medium-high heat. Add onion and sauté until transparent, about 5 minutes. Stir in flour and cook until smooth, about 3 minutes. Gradually add chicken broth, stirring until smooth. Add milk and tomatoes. Bring mixture to a boil, reduce heat and simmer 10 minutes, stirring occasionally. Add cheese and salt. Continue cooking until cheese melts, stirring occasionally. Serve hot.

Yield: 6 to 8 servings.

Vegetable Borscht

New twist on an old European favorite.

1 medium onion, halved

1 medium carrot, peeled

1 medium turnip, peeled and quartered

½ head cabbage, quartered

1 pound potatoes, peeled and quartered

1 pound beets, peeled

1 tablespoon oil

1 clove garlic, minced

1 large tomato, seeded and chopped

7 cups beef broth

1 tablespoon red wine vinegar

Sour cream

Assemble and attach Rotor Slicer/Shredder using thin slicer cone (No 4). Turn to Speed 4 and slice onion, carrot, turnip, cabbage, and potatoes, keeping each separate. Exchange thin slicer cone for coarse shredder cone (No. 2). Turn to Speed 4 and shred beets.

Heat oil in a 5-quart pot over medium heat. Add onion and garlic, and sauté 3 minutes. Add carrot, turnip, beets, tomato, beef broth, and vinegar. Bring mixture to a boil, reduce heat and simmer 30 minutes.

Add cabbage and potatoes and continue to simmer 25 minutes or until vegetables are tender. Serve hot with sour cream.

Yield: 8 to 10 servings.

Minestrone

A robust soup, laden with fresh vegetables.
Perfect for a cold, blustery day.

4 carrots, peeled
2 stalks celery
4 zucchini, trimmed and
  halved lengthwise
2 potatoes, peeled and
  quartered
¼ cup butter or
  margarine
¼ cup olive oil
2 leeks, sliced
2 cloves garlic, minced
2 cans (16 oz. each)
  Italian tomatoes,
  coarsely chopped,
  juice reserved
2 teaspoons salt
¾ teaspoon oregano
¾ teaspoon basil
½ teaspoon rosemary
3 quarts water
2 beef bouillon cubes
2 cans (16 oz. each)
  white beans, drained
  Parmesan cheese

Assemble and attach Rotor Slicer/Shredder using thick slicer cone (No. 3). Turn to Speed 4 and slice carrots, celery, zucchini, and potatoes, keeping each separate.

Heat butter and oil in a 6-quart pot over medium heat. Add carrots, celery, leeks, and garlic and saute 5 minutes. Add zucchini, potatoes, tomatoes with juice, salt, oregano, basil, and rosemary to pot. Cover and simmer 20 minutes, stirring occasionally.

Add water, bouillon cubes, and beans. Bring to a boil; reduce heat, cover and simmer 2 hours. Serve hot with Parmesan cheese.

Yield: 10 to 12 servings.

Potato Leek Soup

Voilà, vichyssoise.

2 pounds potatoes,
  peeled and quartered
2 leeks, trimmed and
  cut into 1-inch pieces
4 cups water
1 teaspoon salt
¼ teaspoon pepper
½ cup milk
1 cup heavy cream

Combine potatoes, leeks, water, salt, and pepper in a 5-quart pot. Cook over medium heat for 25 minutes or until vegetables are tender. Drain vegetables, reserving cooking liquid.

Assemble and attach Fruit/Vegetable Strainer. Turn to Speed 4 and strain potatoes and leeks. Combine strained mixture and reserved liquid; return to pot.

Add milk and heavy cream. Heat through, but do not boil. Refrigerate until well chilled.

Yield: 6 servings.

Cabbage Soup

3 medium potatoes,
  peeled
4 medium carrots,
  peeled
2 medium onions
1 head cabbage
¼ pound bacon, cut into
  1-inch pieces
7 cups water
2 beef bouillon cubes
2 cloves garlic, minced
1 teaspoon chervil
½ teaspoon thyme
2 teaspoons salt
¼ teaspoon pepper

Assemble and attach Rotor Slicer/Shredder using thin slicer cone (No. 1). Turn to Speed 4 and slice potatoes, carrots, onions, and cabbage, keeping each separate.

Fry bacon in 5-quart pot over medium-high heat until crisp. Remove bacon from pot; set aside. Add potatoes, carrots, and onions to pot and sauté 5 minutes or until onions are transparent. Add water and bouillon cubes; reduce heat and simmer 30 minutes. Add cabbage, garlic, chervil, thyme, salt, and pepper. Cover and simmer 1 hour, or until vegetables are very tender.

Place ⅓ of hot mixture in bowl. Attach bowl and wire whip. Turn to Speed 2 and beat until fairly smooth. Repeat with remaining mixture. Return to pot and heat through. Serve hot and garnish with reserved bacon.

Yield: 6 to 8 servings.

Cream of Broccoli Soup

2 packages (10 oz. each)
  frozen, chopped
  broccoli, cooked and
  drained
¼ cup butter or
  margarine
2 tablespoons minced
  onion
2 stalks celery, minced
⅓ cup all-purpose flour
4 cups chicken broth
2 cups milk
  Salt and pepper

Assemble and attach Fruit/Vegetable Strainer. Turn to Speed 4 and strain broccoli. Set aside.

Melt butter in a 5-quart pot over medium heat. Add onion and celery and sauté until tender. Add flour and cook until a smooth paste forms. Add broth and cook until thickened, stirring occasionally. Stir in broccoli, milk, salt, and pepper. Heat through. Serve immediately.

Yield: 6 servings.

Homemade soups take on added appeal when served with an interesting garnish: a spoonful of fresh chopped chives, a thin slice of lemon, a carrot curl, a dab of sour cream, or a spoonful of your own homemade croutons.

Split Pea Soup

A hearty dash of horseradish flavors this perennial favorite.

⅓ *pound bacon, cut into 1-inch pieces*
1 *pound potatoes, peeled and quartered*
2 *stalks celery, cut into 1-inch pieces*
1 *onion, cut into sixths*
1 *leek, trimmed and cut into 1-inch pieces*
¾ *pound dried split peas*
3½ *cups chicken broth*
3 *cups water*
1 *beef bouillon cube*
1 *teaspoon salt*
¼ *teaspoon thyme*
⅛ *teaspoon pepper*
1 *tablespoon horse-radish (optional)*

Cook bacon in 5-quart pot over medium heat until crisp. Remove bacon and set aside; drain half of bacon fat. In remaining fat, sauté potatoes, celery, onion, and leek 3 to 4 minutes or until onion is transparent.

Add peas, chicken broth, water, beef bouillon cube, salt, thyme, and pepper. Reduce heat, cover and simmer 2½ hours. Drain vegetables, reserving cooking liquid.

Assemble and attach Fruit/Vegetable Strainer. Turn to Speed 4 and strain vegetables. Combine strained mixture with reserved liquid and return to pot. Stir in horseradish and heat through. Serve hot with reserved bacon.

Yield: 6 to 8 servings.

Stracciatella

Rome's famous scrambled egg soup.

4 *eggs*
⅔ *cup Parmesan cheese*
¼ *cup chopped parsley*
⅛ *teaspoon nutmeg*
Dash pepper
2 *quarts chicken stock*

Place eggs in bowl. Attach bowl and wire whip. Turn to Speed 6 and whip 1 minute. Add Parmesan cheese, parsley, nutmeg, and pepper. Turn to Speed 4 and whip 30 seconds.

Heat chicken stock in 3-quart saucepan over high heat to a full rolling boil. While stirring stock constantly, gradually add egg mixture until incorporated completely. Serve immediately.

Yield: 8 servings.

Carrot Soup

2 tablespoons butter
  or margarine
5 medium carrots,
  peeled and cut into
  1-inch pieces
1 medium onion, cut
  into sixths
1 large potato, peeled
  and cut into sixths
4 cups chicken broth
½ cup milk
¼ teaspoon basil
¼ teaspoon mace
⅛ teaspoon celery salt

Heat butter in a 3-quart saucepan over medium heat. Add carrots and onion and sauté 5 minutes or until onion is transparent. Add potatoes and chicken broth and bring to a boil. Reduce heat, cover and simmer for 30 minutes or until potatoes are soft.

Drain cooked vegetables, reserving cooking liquid. Assemble and attach Fruit/Vegetable Strainer. Turn to Speed 4 and strain vegetables. Return strained vegetables and cooking liquid to pan. Add milk, basil, mace, and celery salt. Heat through but do not boil. Serve hot.

Yield: 6 servings.

Lentil Soup

Serve this hearty soup with a sprinkling of fresh lemon juice
and your favorite dark bread.

1 onion, quartered
3 carrots, peeled and
  halved lengthwise
2 stalks celery, halved
  lengthwise
5 slices bacon, cut into
  1-inch pieces
1 clove garlic, minced
7 cups water
2 cups lentils
1 chicken bouillon cube
2 teaspoons salt
¼ teaspoon pepper
⅛ teaspoon thyme
1 bay leaf
1 lemon, juiced

Assemble and attach Rotor Slicer/Shredder using thick slicer cone (No. 3). Turn to Speed 4 and slice onion, carrots, and celery; set aside.

Fry bacon in a 5-quart pot over medium heat until crisp. Remove from pot and set aside. Add onion, carrots, celery, and garlic to pot and sauté 4 minutes or until tender.

Add water, lentils, chicken bouillon cube, salt, pepper, thyme, bay leaf, and lemon juice. Cover and simmer 3 hours, or until lentils are tender. Serve hot; garnish with reserved bacon.

Yield: 6 to 8 servings.

Gazpacho

Refresh yourself on a hot summer's day with this cool blend
of fresh tomatoes and other garden vegetables.

4 slices white bread

4 tablespoons olive oil

1 clove garlic, minced

*7 large very ripe
tomatoes, cut into
sixths*

1 onion, quartered

*1 cucumber, peeled,
seeded and cut into
sixths*

*1 green pepper, seeded
and cut into sixths*

*2 tablespoons wine
vinegar*

*1 teaspoon Worcester-
shire sauce*

1 teaspoon salt

*⅛ teaspoon pepper
Hot pepper sauce to
taste*

Trim crusts from bread and cut into ½-inch cubes. Heat
3 tablespoons oil in a 12-inch skillet. Add garlic and saute
1 minute. Add bread cubes and saute 4 minutes. Spread
bread cubes on a baking sheet. Bake at 350°F for 20 to 30
minutes or until crisp; set aside.

Assemble and attach Fruit/Vegetable Strainer. Turn to
Speed 4 and strain 5 tomatoes into a large bowl.

Assemble and attach Food Grinder using coarse grinding
plate. Turn to Speed 4 and grind remaining tomatoes,
onion, cucumber, and green pepper into bowl with tomato
puree. Add remaining olive oil, vinegar, Worcestershire
sauce, salt, pepper, and hot pepper sauce; mix well.
Refrigerate at least 2 hours before serving. Serve with
toasted bread cubes.

Yield: 6 servings.

SAUCES DRESSINGS & RELISHES

Pulling it all together

The simplest of meals take on a special touch
when you serve them with homemade salad
dressings, sauces, and relishes. Select from an
assortment of dressings and sauces to enhance
your favorite fruits and vegetables, or enjoy
their goodness all year-round in preserved
relishes. Each one is decidedly better tasting
than store-bought varieties, and surprisingly
simple to make.

Mayonnaise

3 egg yolks 2 cups vegetable or olive oil 1 lemon, juiced 1 teaspoon salt ¼ teaspoon dry mustard 1 tablespoon cider vinegar	Place egg yolks in bowl. Attach bowl and wire whip. Turn to Speed 10 and whip about 3 minutes, or until yolks are stiff and pale yellow. Reduce to Speed 8 and slowly add 1 cup oil, a teaspoon at a time, in a thin stream. If mixture becomes too thick, thin with lemon juice. Carefully add remaining oil in a *slow, steady* stream until completely absorbed. Reduce to Speed 6, add lemon juice, salt, dry mustard, and vinegar, and whip just until blended. Store mayonnaise in refrigerator. *Yield:* 2½ cups.

Mayonnaise Variations

Dill Mayonnaise

Especially good on garden-fresh tomatoes and cucumbers.

1 cup mayonnaise 1 teaspoon dried dill weed 1 tablespoon lemon juice ¼ teaspoon pepper	Place all ingredients in bowl. Attach bowl and flat beater. Turn to Speed 2 and mix 1 minute. Chill thoroughly before serving. *Yield:* 1 cup.

Russian Dressing

The freshness of this homemade dressing makes an incomparable difference.

1 cup mayonnaise ½ cup catsup 2 drops hot pepper sauce ¼ cup chopped parsley Salt and pepper	Place all ingredients in bowl. Attach bowl and flat beater. Turn to Speed 2 and mix 1 minute. Chill thoroughly before serving. *Yield:* 1½ cups.

Bleu Cheese Dressing
A time-honored topping laden with chunks of fresh bleu cheese.

1 cup mayonnaise
⅔ cup crumbled Bleu
 cheese
2 tablespoons lemon
 juice
¼ teaspoon pepper

Place all ingredients in bowl. Attach bowl and flat beater. Turn to Stir Speed and mix 1 minute. Chill thoroughly before serving.

Yield: 2 cups.

If mayonnaise should separate, beat a fresh, warm egg yolk in mixer bowl for 1 minute using the wire whip. Beat in a few drops of oil, then a teaspoon of the separated mayonnaise. As the new sauce comes together, add the separated mayonnaise in increasing amounts until all of it has been incorporated.

Creole Sauce
Try this spicy Louisiana favorite in your next omelet or over baked fish.

3 large tomatoes, cut
 into sixths
2 tablespoons olive oil
1 large onion, diced
1 large green pepper,
 seeded and diced
3 stalks celery, diced
1 cup sliced
 mushrooms
2 large tomatoes,
 seeded and diced
1 bay leaf
3 drops hot pepper
 sauce

Assemble and attach Fruit/Vegetable Strainer. Turn to Speed 4 and puree cut tomatoes; set aside.

Heat oil in 12-inch skillet over medium-high heat. Add onion, green pepper, and celery. Sauté about 5 minutes, or until transparent.

Add tomato puree, mushrooms, diced tomatoes, bay leaf, and hot pepper sauce. Reduce heat, cover and simmer 20 minutes. Remove bay leaf before serving. Use sauce as a topping for baked fish or poultry or as an omelet filling.

Yield: 2½ cups.

Cucumber Sauce

Great on broiled fish, baked potatoes or as a new
and different dressing for greens.

3 large cucumbers,
 peeled, seeded and
 cut into 1-inch pieces
1 teaspoon dried dill
 weed
1 teaspoon salt
⅛ teaspoon pepper
2 tablespoons lemon
 juice
½ cup sour cream

Assemble and attach Food Grinder using fine grinding
plate. Turn to Speed 4 and grind cucumbers. Drain excess
juice.

Place cucumbers in a bowl and add dill weed, salt,
pepper, and lemon juice; mix well. Fold in sour cream
and chill thoroughly.

Yield: 2 cups.

Zucchini Relish

10 medium zucchini,
 trimmed and cut into
 eighths
4 medium green
 peppers, seeded and
 cut into sixths
3 medium sweet red
 peppers, seeded and
 cut into sixths
6 medium onions, cut
 into sixths
5 tablespoons salt
 Water
2½ cups distilled white
 vinegar
2½ cups sugar
1 teaspoon turmeric
1 teaspoon nutmeg
1 teaspoon dry mustard
2 teaspoons celery salt

Assemble and attach Food Grinder using coarse grinding
plate. Turn to Speed 4 and grind zucchini, peppers, and
onion into a large bowl. Cover ground vegetables with
salt and water; let stand overnight.

Rinse and drain vegetables and place in a 5-quart pot.
Add vinegar, sugar, turmeric, nutmeg, dry mustard, and
celery salt. Bring mixture to a boil; reduce heat and simmer
30 minutes. Ladle into hot, sterilized jars and process
15 minutes in boiling water bath. Remove jars from bath;
cool and check seals.

Yield: 5 pints.

Horseradish Sauce

Adds a provocative zing to smoked fish or broiled beef.

1 cup heavy cream 3 tablespoons horseradish ¼ teaspoon salt ¼ cup chopped parsley	Place cream in bowl. Attach bowl and wire whip. Turn to Speed 8 and whip until stiff peaks form. Reduce to Speed 2 and add horseradish, salt, and parsley, mixing just until combined. Serve immediately. *Yield:* 2 cups.

Apple Relish

An unusual combination of onion, red pepper and apples.
Great with German fare.

5 onions, *quartered*

1 teaspoon crushed red pepper

1 cup boiling water

1 tablespoon salt

14 large red apples, cored and quartered

1 quart distilled white vinegar

4 cups sugar

2 teaspoons allspice

1 tablespoon whole cloves

1 stick cinnamon

Assemble and attach Food Grinder using coarse grinding plate. Turn to Speed 4 and grind onions and red pepper into a small bowl. Add water and salt. Let stand 15 minutes, then drain.

Attach clean Food Grinder with coarse grinding plate. Grind apples into a 5-quart pot. Add onion and red pepper, vinegar, sugar, and cloth bag filled with spices. Bring to a boil and cook 15 minutes. Remove spice bag. Ladle into hot, sterilized jars and process 15 minutes in boiling water bath. Remove jars from bath; cool and check seals.

Yield: 6 pints.

Herbed Dressing

⅔ cup cider vinegar
1½ teaspoons salt
½ teaspoon pepper
½ teaspoon dry mustard
¼ teaspoon tarragon
¼ teaspoon basil
¼ teaspoon chervil
1½ cups vegetable oil or
    olive oil

Place vinegar, salt, pepper, dry mustard, tarragon, basil, and chervil in bowl. Attach bowl and wire whip. Turn to Speed 6 and whip for 2 minutes.

Increase to Speed 8 and slowly add oil in a thin, steady stream until absorbed. Chill thoroughly. Note: Dressing may separate. Shake well before serving.

Yield: 2 cups.

Poppy Seed Dressing

¼ cup sugar
⅓ cup cider vinegar
1 teaspoon dry mustard
1 teaspoon minced
    onion
1 teaspoon salt
1 cup vegetable oil
1½ teaspoons poppy
    seeds

Place sugar, vinegar, dry mustard, onion, and salt in bowl. Attach bowl and wire whip. Turn to Speed 4 and whip for 2 minutes.

Increase to Speed 8 and slowly add oil in a thin, steady stream until completely absorbed. Reduce to Stir Speed and add poppy seeds, mixing just until combined. Chill thoroughly before serving.

Yield: 1½ cups.

Peach Chutney

Akin to the mango chutney of India, this is a fine accompaniment to dishes seasoned with curry.

12 firm peaches, halved
   and pitted
3 sweet peppers, seeded
   and quartered
1 large onion, halved
⅞ cup cider vinegar
¾ cup sugar
½ clove garlic, minced
½ teaspoon salt
½ cup raisins
½ navel orange,
   quartered
½ lemon, seeded and
   quartered
⅛ cup chopped
   crystallized ginger
½ teaspoon ground
   ginger

Assemble and attach Rotor Slicer/Shredder using thick slicer cone (No. 3). Turn to Speed 4 and slice peaches, peppers, and onion; set aside.

Heat 1¼ cups vinegar and sugar in an 8-quart pot over medium heat. Bring mixture to a boil, reduce heat and simmer 10 minutes.

Add peaches, peppers, onions, garlic, salt, and raisins to pot. Simmer, stirring frequently, for 10 minutes.

Assemble and attach Food Grinder using coarse grinding plate. Turn to Speed 4 and grind orange and lemon. Add ground fruit and crystallized ginger to pot; simmer 30 minutes, stirring occasionally.

Add remaining vinegar and ground ginger to mixture. Simmer 1 hour or until thick, stirring occasionally. Ladle mixture into hot sterilized jars and seal. Process 15 minutes in boiling water bath. Remove jars from bath; cool and check seals.

Yield: 6 pints.

Red Pepper Relish

This spicy condiment can also be served as an hors d'oeuvre
over cream cheese and your favorite crackers.

2 large tomatoes, cut
　　into eighths
2 stalks celery, cut into
　　1-inch pieces
3 red peppers, seeded
　　and cut into eighths
1 onion, quartered
1 tablespoon salt
2 tablespoons sugar
⅛ teaspoon allspice
⅛ teaspoon cinnamon
⅛ teaspoon cloves
¼ cup red wine vinegar

Assemble and attach Fruit/Vegetable Strainer. Turn to
Speed 4 and strain tomatoes into a large glass bowl.

Assemble and attach Food Grinder using coarse grinding
plate. Turn to Speed 4 and grind celery, peppers, and
onion into glass bowl. Add salt, sugar, allspice, cinnamon,
cloves, and vinegar; mix well.

Cover and refrigerate, stirring occasionally, at least
8 hours before serving.

Yield: 4 cups.

To sterilize jars: Wash jars in hot, sudsy water and rinse well. Put jars in
a large kettle and cover with hot water. Bring to a boil and boil for 15
minutes. Turn off heat and let jars stand in hot water until ready to fill.
Sterilize lids for 5 minutes, or according to manufacturer's directions.

Orange Fluff Sauce

A first-rate idea to grace a fruit salad or simple cake.

2 tablespoons flour
½ cup sugar
1 can (6 oz.) frozen
　　orange juice, thawed
¾ cup water
1 cup heavy cream

Combine flour, sugar, orange juice and water in a small
saucepan. Heat mixture over medium heat, stirring
constantly until thick and smooth, about 5 minutes.
Cool mixture 1 hour, stirring occasionally.

Place cream in bowl. Attach bowl and wire whip. Turn
to Speed 8 and whip until stiff peaks form. Fold orange
mixture into whipped cream. Serve immediately.

Yield: 2½ cups.

Eggnog Sauce

Bestow this rich rum and nutmeg topping on warm gingerbread.

*1 package (¾ oz.)
  vanilla pudding mix*
2 cups milk
⅛ teaspoon nutmeg
½ cup heavy cream
2 tablespoons dark rum

Place pudding mix in a 2-quart saucepan and gradually add milk. Cook over medium heat, stirring constantly, until smooth and thick. Stir in nutmeg and remove from heat. Cool to lukewarm.

Place cream in bowl. Attach bowl and wire whip. Turn to Speed 8 and whip until stiff. Reduce to Speed 2 and add pudding and rum, mixing just until blended. Serve warm.

Yield: 2 cups.

Rémoulade Sauce

A piquant blend of capers, Dijon mustard and your own mayonnaise.
Good accompaniment to cold meat, poultry and shellfish.

1 cup mayonnaise
*3 tablespoons chopped
  capers*
*1 tablespoon chopped
  dill pickle*
½ teaspoon tarragon
½ teaspoon chervil
¼ teaspoon salt
¼ teaspoon pepper
*2 teaspoons Dijon-style
  mustard*

Place all ingredients in bowl. Attach bowl and wire whip. Turn to Speed 4 and whip 1 minute. Chill thoroughly before serving.

Yield: 1 cup.

Tomato Mousse

Smooth and spicy; a summer treat to serve with fish or meat.

3 large tomatoes, cut into sixths
1 teaspoon salt
2 teaspoons Worcestershire sauce
¼ teaspoon pepper
½ teaspoon chervil
¼ teaspoon basil
2 teaspoons sugar
2 packages (¼ oz. each) gelatin
½ cup water
1 cup heavy cream

Assemble and attach Fruit/Vegetable Strainer. Turn to Speed 4 and strain tomatoes. Combine strained tomatoes, salt, Worcestershire sauce, pepper, chervil, basil, and sugar and set aside.

Sprinkle gelatin over water; let stand 5 minutes to soften. Completely dissolve gelatin over hot water. Add dissolved gelatin to tomato mixture and mix well. Chill mixture until partially set.

Place cream in bowl. Attach bowl and wire whip. Turn to Speed 8 and whip until stiff. Fold tomato mixture into whipped cream and pour into an oiled 4-cup mold. Refrigerate until set. When ready to serve, unmold onto serving platter.

Yield: 6 to 8 servings.

Grated Carrot Casserole

High on nutrition and easy on the budget.

5 carrots, peeled
1 cup long grain rice
2 tablespoons minced onion
½ teaspoon salt
¼ teaspoon pepper
2 cups water
½ pound American cheese
1 cup milk
2 eggs, beaten
⅛ teaspoon nutmeg

Assemble and attach Rotor Slicer/Shredder using coarse shredder cone (No. 2). Turn to Speed 4 and shred carrots. Combine carrots, rice, onion, salt, pepper, and water in large saucepan. Bring to a boil, then reduce heat; cover and simmer 25 minutes.

Exchange coarse shredder cone for fine shredder cone (No. 1). Turn to Speed 4 and shred cheese. Combine cheese, milk, eggs, and nutmeg and pour over carrot and rice mixture; mix well. Place in 1½-quart casserole dish and bake at 350°F for 30 to 40 minutes. Serve immediately.

Yield: 6 to 8 servings.

Marinated Cucumber Salad

4 cucumbers, trimmed
   and peeled
2 small onions, halved
   lengthwise
½ cup white vinegar
½ cup water
2 teaspoons sugar
1 teaspoon dried dill
½ teaspoon salt
⅛ teaspoon pepper

Assemble and attach Rotor Slicer/Shredder using thin slicer cone (No. 4). Turn to Speed 4 and slice cucumbers and onions into a large bowl.

Add vinegar, water, sugar, dill, salt, and pepper. Toss gently to mix. Cover mixture and refrigerate at least 3 hours before serving.

Yield: 6 to 8 servings.

Turnip and Squash Mousseline

Pleasing combination of turnip and acorn squash, whipped into perfection with heavy cream and nutmeg, then topped with a sprinkling of bread crumbs and melted butter.

2 pounds turnips,
   peeled and cut into
   1-inch cubes
2 acorn squash, peeled
   and cut into 1-inch
   cubes
1 cup heavy cream
1 egg
⅛ teaspoon nutmeg
2 teaspoons salt
¼ teaspoon pepper
½ cup fresh bread
   crumbs
2 tablespoons butter or
   margarine, melted

Place turnips and squash in large 5-quart pot and cover with water. Bring to a boil over medium heat, then reduce heat and simmer 20 minutes or until vegetables are tender; drain.

Assemble and attach Fruit/Vegetable Strainer. Turn to Speed 4 and strain turnips and squash into bowl. Add cream, egg, nutmeg, salt, and pepper. Attach bowl and wire whip. Turn to Speed 2 and whip 30 seconds. Stop and scrape bowl. Turn to Speed 2 and whip for another 30 seconds.

Place mixture in a greased 1½-quart casserole dish. Sprinkle bread crumbs on top and drizzle with melted butter. Bake at 350°F for 45 to 50 minutes. Serve immediately.

Yield: 6 servings.

Braised Red Cabbage

The perfect complement to roast pork, duck or goose.

1 small head red
   cabbage
1 onion
¼ cup sugar
1 tablespoon salt
1 cup red wine vinegar
¼ cup butter or
   margarine
1 apple, peeled, cored
   and diced
½ cup red currant jelly
¼ cup hot water
⅛ teaspoon cloves
¼ teaspoon cinnamon

Assemble and attach Rotor Slicer/Shredder using thin slicer cone (No. 4). Turn to Speed 4 and slice cabbage and onion, keeping each separate. Combine cabbage, sugar, salt, and vinegar in a large bowl and marinate 15 minutes.

Melt butter in 5-quart pot over medium heat. Add onion and sauté 5 minutes or until transparent. Add apple and sauté 5 more minutes. Add cabbage mixture to pot and bring to a boil; reduce heat.

Combine jelly, hot water, cloves, and cinnamon. Add to cabbage mixture. Cover and simmer 1 hour or until tender. Serve immediately.

Yield: 6 to 8 servings.

Vegetables Oriental Style

A surefire stir-fry.

4 stalks celery
1 bunch broccoli,
   flowerets trimmed,
   stems peeled and
   reserved
2 onions, halved
12 mushrooms
1 clove garlic
¼ cup peanut or
   vegetable oil
1 tablespoon sherry
¼ teaspoon ground
   ginger
1 tablespoon soy sauce

Assemble and attach Rotor Slicer/Shredder using thick slicer cone (No. 3). Turn to Speed 4 and slice celery, broccoli stems, onions, and mushrooms, keeping each separate.

Heat half of oil in a 12-inch skillet or wok over medium-high heat. Add celery, onions, and garlic and stir-fry 1 minute. Add sherry and cook 30 seconds. Remove from pan.

Heat remaining oil in pan. Add broccoli flowerets and stir-fry 1 minute. Add sliced broccoli stems and stir-fry until not quite tender, about 2 minutes. Add mushrooms and stir-fry 1 minute.

Return celery, onions, and garlic to pan. Stir-fry until hot. Season with ground ginger and soy sauce and serve immediately.

Yield: 6 servings.

Spinach Soufflé

2 packages (10 oz. each) frozen chopped spinach, cooked
¼ pound Cheddar cheese
¼ cup butter or margarine
1 tablespoon minced onion
5 tablespoons flour
1 cup milk
1 teaspoon salt
¼ teaspoon pepper
⅛ teaspoon nutmeg
3 eggs, separated

Wring spinach in towel until very dry. Assemble and attach Food Grinder using coarse grinding plate. Turn to Speed 4 and grind spinach; set aside.

Assemble and attach Rotor Slicer/Shredder using fine shredder cone (No. 1). Turn to Speed 4 and shred cheese; set aside.

Melt butter in saucepan over medium heat. Add onion and sauté 5 minutes. Blend in flour, then gradually add milk, stirring until smooth. Continue cooking until thickened, about 5 minutes. Remove mixture from heat and stir in spinach, cheese, salt, pepper, and nutmeg; set aside.

Place egg whites in bowl. Attach bowl and wire whip. Turn to Speed 8 and whip until stiff but not dry. Remove egg whites from bowl.

Place egg yolks in clean bowl. Attach bowl and wire whip. Turn to Speed 4 and whip egg yolks until thick, about 1 minute.

Fold spinach and cheese mixture into beaten egg whites, then fold in beaten egg yolks. Pour into a greased 1½-quart souffle dish and bake at 350°F for 45 to 50 minutes. Serve immediately.

Yield: 4 to 6 servings.

Green Pepper Aspic
Something special . . . for green pepper!

4 large green peppers,
  seeded and cut into
  sixths
⅓ cup water
1 package (¼ oz.)
  gelatin
1 tablespoon lemon
  juice
1 teaspoon salt
¼ teaspoon pepper
1 carrot, peeled
1 cup mayonnaise

Assemble and attach Food Grinder using fine grinding plate. Turn to Speed 4 and grind peppers; measure out ¼ cup pepper juice. Place juice and water in saucepan. Heat over medium heat to boil; remove from heat and sprinkle gelatin over mixture. Stir well to dissolve completely. Add lemon juice, salt, and pepper and mix well. Refrigerate until partially set.

Assemble and attach Rotor Slicer/Shredder using fine shredder cone (No. 1). Turn to Speed 4 and shred carrots. Mix carrots, remaining green peppers, and mayonnaise together. Fold into gelatin mixture. Place mixture in an oiled 4-cup mold. Refrigerate until set. Unmold before serving.

Yield: 6 servings.

Ratatouille

1 eggplant, trimmed
2 teaspoons salt
2 medium zucchini,
  trimmed
3 onions, halved
  lengthwise
2 green peppers, halved
  and seeded
⅓ cup olive oil
2 cloves garlic, minced
4 large tomatoes, peeled,
  seeded and diced
¼ cup chopped fresh
  parsley
1 bay leaf
¼ teaspoon oregano
¼ teaspoon basil
¼ teaspoon pepper

Cut eggplant lengthwise into quarters. Cut each quarter crosswise into ¼-inch slices. Sprinkle with salt and let stand 30 minutes. Rinse, drain, and pat eggplant dry with paper towel.

Assemble and attach Rotor Slicer/Shredder using thick slicer cone (No. 3). Turn to Speed 4 and slice zucchini, onions, and green pepper, keeping each separate.

Heat olive oil in large 5-quart pot over medium heat. Add onions, green pepper, and garlic and sauté 10 minutes. Add eggplant and zucchini; mix gently, reduce heat, cover and simmer 20 minutes.

Add tomatoes, parsley, bay leaf, oregano, basil, and pepper. Cover and simmer 30 minutes. Remove cover and simmer 15 minutes to absorb excess liquid. Serve hot or cold.

Yield: 6 to 8 servings.

Stuffed Eggplant

3 medium eggplants,
trimmed
2 small onions,
quartered
2 cloves garlic
¼ cup olive oil
¾ cup long grain rice
1 can (10¾ oz.) chicken
broth
1 teaspoon sugar
½ teaspoon basil
½ teaspoon salt
½ teaspoon pepper
Dash cinnamon
2 tomatoes, diced
½ cup Parmesan cheese
2 tablespoons butter or
margarine, melted

Cut eggplants in half lengthwise. Scoop out pulp, leaving a ⅜-inch shell; set aside.

Assemble and attach Food Grinder using coarse grinding plate. Turn to Speed 4 and grind eggplant pulp, onions, and garlic.

Heat oil in a 12-inch skillet over medium heat. Add ground vegetables and sauté 4 minutes. Add rice, chicken broth, sugar, basil, salt, pepper, and cinnamon; mix well. Cover and simmer over low heat for 15 minutes. Add tomatoes and simmer 10 minutes more.

Remove mixture from heat and stir in Parmesan cheese. Loosely stuff each eggplant shell. Place shells in a greased 9 x 13 x 2-inch pan. Brush with butter. Cover and bake at 325 °F for 20 minutes. Remove cover and bake 30 minutes more or until tops are crusty. Serve immediately.

Yield: 6 servings.

When selecting eggplant, they should be firm, with a shiny, smooth purple skin.

Sweet Potato Puff

For the holidays and other movable feasts.

2 medium sweet
  potatoes, cooked and
  peeled
½ cup milk
¾ cup sugar
2 eggs
⅓ cup butter or
  margarine
½ teaspoon nutmeg
½ teaspoon cinnamon

Place sweet potatoes in bowl. Attach bowl and wire whip. Turn to Speed 2 and beat for 30 seconds. Add milk, sugar, eggs, butter, nutmeg, and cinnamon. Turn to Speed 4 and beat for 1 minute. Spread mixture into a greased 9-inch pie plate. Bake at 400°F for 20 minutes or until set. Spread *Crunchy Praline Topping* over hot sweet potatoes. Bake an additional 10 minutes. Serve immediately.

Yield: 6 servings.

Crunchy Praline Topping

⅓ cup butter or
  margarine, melted
¾ cup cornflake cereal
½ cup chopped nuts
½ cup brown sugar

Place all ingredients in bowl. Attach bowl and flat beater. Turn to Stir Speed and mix for 15 seconds.

Tomato Cheese Tart

3 large tomatoes, sliced
  ½-inch thick
2 teaspoons salt
1 pound provolone
  cheese
1 egg white, beaten
1 teaspoon basil
2 tablespoons
  Parmesan cheese
2 teaspoons olive oil
  KitchenAid Pie
  Pastry for 9-inch
  double-crust pie

Sprinkle tomatoes with salt and drain on a rack for 30 minutes.

Roll out pastry to ⅛-inch thickness and line an 11-inch quiche/flan pan. Fill with pastry weights and bake at 450°F for 10 to 12 minutes, or until lightly browned. Remove pastry weights and cool.

Assemble and attach Rotor Slicer/Shredder using fine shredder cone (No.1). Turn to Speed 4 and shred provolone cheese. Brush bottom and sides of pastry shell with egg white. Place provolone cheese in shell and top with tomatoes. Sprinkle basil and Parmesan cheese over tomatoes; and drizzle with olive oil.

Bake at 375°F for 25 to 30 minutes, or until cheese has melted and tomatoes are tender. Serve immediately.

Yield: 6 to 8 servings.

Mélange of Squash

A colorful sauté of garden-fresh vegetables.

2 medium zucchini, trimmed
1 medium yellow squash, trimmed
2 large carrots, peeled
¼ cup butter or margarine
½ teaspoon salt
½ teaspoon pepper
1 lemon, juiced

Assemble and attach Rotor Slicer/Shredder using coarse shredder cone (No. 2). Turn to Speed 4 and shred zucchini, yellow squash, and carrots.

Melt butter in 10-inch skillet over medium-high heat. Add vegetables and quickly sauté, about 3 minutes. Add salt, pepper, and lemon juice and toss gently. Serve immediately.

Yield: 4 to 6 servings.

Bacon Swiss Potatoes

A cheesy, crunchy and satisfying way to dress up potatoes.

3-4 potatoes, peeled and halved
1 medium onion
½ pound Swiss cheese
6 slices bacon
4 eggs, beaten
¾ cup heavy cream
¼ teaspoon nutmeg
½ teaspoon salt
¼ teaspoon pepper
1 clove garlic, minced

Assemble and attach Rotor Slicer/Shredder using coarse shredder cone (No. 2). Turn to Speed 4 and shred potatoes and onion, keeping each separate. Set aside.

Exchange coarse shredder cone for fine shredder cone (No. 1). Turn to Speed 4 and shred cheese. Set aside.

Fry bacon in a 12-inch skillet over medium-high heat until very crisp. Remove from pan and crumble. Drain all but ¼ cup bacon fat. Add onion and sauté 3 minutes; set aside.

Combine 2 cups shredded cheese, eggs, heavy cream, nutmeg, salt, pepper, and garlic in a medium saucepan. Cook over low heat, stirring occasionally, until cheese melts. Do not boil. Add potatoes and mix well.

Pour half of cheese/potato mixture into a greased 9 x 9 x 1½-inch pan. Sprinkle half of bacon over mixture. Repeat with remaining cheese/potato mixture and bacon. Top with remaining cheese. Bake at 400°F for 45 to 50 minutes, or until bubbly and golden brown. Serve immediately.

Yield: 6 to 8 servings.

Curried Cabbage

Steamed cabbage in a creamy sauce lightly seasoned with curry.

½ medium head
   cabbage, quartered
4 tablespoons butter or
   margarine
4 tablespoons all-
   purpose flour
Dash pepper
½ teaspoon curry
   powder
2 tablespoons minced
   onion
1 teaspoon salt
¾ cup milk

Assemble and attach Rotor Slicer/Shredder using thin slicer cone (No. 4). Turn to Speed 4 and slice cabbage. Steam cabbage over boiling water just until tender.

Melt butter in a double boiler over boiling water. Stir in flour, pepper, curry powder, onion, and salt. Gradually add milk, stirring constantly, until smooth. Continue cooking until thickened. Do not boil.

Place cabbage in a serving dish and add sauce. Toss well to coat cabbage. Serve immediately.

Yield: 6 to 8 servings.

Broccoli-Cheese Bake

1 package (10 oz.)
   frozen chopped
   broccoli, cooked and
   well drained
1 small onion,
   quartered
½ pound Cheddar
   cheese
1 cup all-purpose flour
1 teaspoon salt
1 teaspoon baking
   powder
1 cup milk
2 eggs
⅓ cup butter or
   margarine, melted

Assemble and attach Food Grinder using coarse grinding plate. Turn to Speed 4 and grind broccoli and onion. Set aside.

Assemble and attach Rotor Slicer/Shredder using fine shredder cone (No. 1). Turn to Speed 4 and shred cheese. Set aside.

Sift flour, salt, and baking powder into bowl. Add milk, eggs, and butter. Attach bowl and flat beater. Turn to Speed 2 and mix 1 minute.

Add broccoli mixture and cheese. Turn to Speed 2 and mix 30 seconds. Pour mixture into a greased 9 x 9 x 1½-inch pan. Bake at 375°F for 60 to 75 minutes. Cut into 3-inch squares to serve.

Yield: 6 to 8 servings.

Carrots Lyonnaise

A delicious alternative.

1 pound carrots, peeled
3 medium onions, halved
1 cup chicken broth
4 tablespoons butter or margarine
⅛ teaspoon sugar
1 tablespoon all-purpose flour
¼ teaspoon salt
Dash pepper
Dash nutmeg

Assemble and attach Rotor Slicer/Shredder using thick slicer cone (No. 3). Turn to Speed 4 and slice carrots and onions, keeping each separate.

Place carrots and chicken broth in saucepan. Bring to a boil over medium heat; reduce heat and simmer 10 minutes.

Melt butter in a large skillet over medium heat. Add onions and sugar and sauté 5 minutes, stirring occasionally. Add flour to onions and cook 2 minutes.

Add carrots and broth, salt, pepper, and nutmeg. Bring to a boil; reduce heat and simmer 10 to 15 minutes or until liquid has thickened. Serve immediately.

Yield: 4 to 6 servings.

Carrots will stay fresher longer if tops are removed before storing in vegetable crisper.

Cole Slaw

1 medium head cabbage, quartered
2 carrots, peeled
1 green pepper, seeded
1½ cups mayonnaise
3 tablespoons white vinegar
1 teaspoon sugar
½ teaspoon salt
¼ teaspoon pepper
¼ cup milk

Assemble and attach Rotor Slicer/Shredder using thin slicer cone (No. 4). Turn to Speed 4 and slice cabbage into a large bowl. Exchange thin slicer cone for coarse shredder cone (No. 2). Turn to Speed 4 and shred carrots and green pepper into large bowl.

Add mayonnaise, vinegar, sugar, salt, pepper, and milk. Thoroughly combine ingredients by hand. Cover and refrigerate at least three hours before serving.

Yield: 8 to 10 servings.

Potato Pancakes

Don't forget to pass along the Sauerbraten and applesauce, too.

3 medium potatoes,
  peeled and halved

1 small onion

3 eggs

2 tablespoons all-
  purpose flour

1 tablespoon chopped
  parsley

1 teaspoon salt
  Dash pepper
  Vegetable oil for
  frying

Assemble and attach Rotor Slicer/Shredder using fine shredder cone (No. 1). Turn to Speed 4 and shred potatoes and onion.

Place eggs in bowl. Attach bowl and flat beater. Turn to Speed 2 and beat 1 minute. Add potatoes, onion, flour, salt, parsley, and pepper. Turn to Stir Speed and mix 30 seconds, until well blended.

Heat a small amount of oil in a 12-inch skillet over medium heat. Use 3 tablespoons of potato mixture for each pancake and drop into hot oil. Fry until golden brown, about 4 to 5 minutes, on each side. Serve immediately.

Yield: 6 servings.

MAIN DISHES

Pièce de résistance

What's for dinner? No matter what else you are serving, the main course remains the sum and substance of your meal. The good cook varies it to avoid boredom, to accommodate seasonal moods, or to set the tone for the entire evening.

In doing so, the main course should provide the balance and proper perspective to a meal. It should be low-keyed when dessert is especially rich. But when the occasion calls for something elaborate, almost sumptuous, the main course should be surrounded by little more than a simple first course and dessert.

The recipes that follow fit into every scheme. There are dishes for a casual buffet and for a grand sit-down dinner. Simple fare like Steamed Mussels with Herbs, and Beef Roulade to an elegant assembly of delicate Quenelles of Sole served with a Piquant Caper Sauce. Whatever the occasion, we guarantee that you and your guests will enjoy the pleasure of your selection.

Chicken and Zucchini Parmesan

1½ pounds zucchini, trimmed

2½ teaspoons salt

3 whole chicken breasts boned, skinned, and split

½ cup all-purpose flour

¼ cup olive oil

¼ teaspoon pepper

1¼ cups Parmesan cheese

1 teaspoon basil

1 teaspoon oregano

⅛ teaspoon nutmeg

2 tablespoons chopped parsley

Assemble and attach Rotor Slicer/Shredder using thick slicer cone (No. 3). Turn to Speed 4 and slice zucchini into a bowl. Sprinkle with 2 teaspoons salt, toss and set aside for 30 minutes. Rinse well and drain.

Pound chicken between wax paper until thin; dredge in flour. Heat oil in a 12-inch skillet over medium heat and brown chicken. Drain and sprinkle with remaining salt and pepper.

Mix 1 cup Parmesan cheese, basil, oregano, nutmeg, and parsley together. Place half of zucchini in a greased 9 x 9 x 2-inch pan; sprinkle with half of cheese mixture. Arrange chicken on zucchini and sprinkle with remaining half of cheese mixture. Top chicken with remaining zucchini and sprinkle with remaining ¼ cup Parmesan cheese. Cover tightly and bake at 325°F for 30 minutes. Uncover and bake 15 minutes longer at 375°F. Serve immediately

Yield: 6 servings.

Mu Shu Pork

Typical Northern Chinese dish of pork, eggs and shredded cabbage.

½ pound boneless pork loin, thinly sliced

1 tablespoon sherry

1 tablespoon soy sauce

1 teaspoon cornstarch

½ teaspoon sugar

¼ teaspoon ground ginger

4 teaspoons vegetable oil

3 eggs, beaten

¼ head cabbage

1 stalk celery

½ cup chopped scallions

1 teaspoon sesame seeds

Combine pork, sherry, soy sauce, cornstarch, sugar, and ground ginger; mix well and set aside.

Heat 2 teaspoons oil in a 12-inch skillet or wok over medium heat. Add eggs and scramble until very dry; break into small pieces. Remove from pan and set aside.

Assemble and attach Rotor Slicer/Shredder using thin slicer cone (No. 4). Turn to Speed 4 and slice cabbage and celery.

Heat remaining oil in pan and add pork mixture. Stir-fry until pork is thoroughly cooked. Add cabbage and celery to pan and stir-fry 2 minutes. Add eggs, scallions, and sesame seeds. Stir-fry 1 minute. Serve immediately.

Yield: 4 servings.

Quenelles of Sole with Caper Cheese Sauce

Light-as-a-cloud fish dumplings served with a snappy cheese sauce.

---

2 pounds sole filets
¼ cup butter or margarine
¾ cup water
1 cup all-purpose flour
3 eggs
¼ teaspoon pepper
1 teaspoon salt
⅛ teaspoon nutmeg
2 teaspoons chopped parsley
2 tablespoons heavy cream
2 teaspoons lemon juice
Boiling water

Assemble and attach Food Grinder using fine grinding plate. Turn to Speed 4 and grind sole 3 times; drain well after each grind. Set aside.

Heat butter and water in saucepan over medium heat. When mixture boils, reduce heat and quickly stir in flour, mixing vigorously until mixture leaves sides of pan in a ball. Place mixture in bowl. Attach bowl and flat beater. Turn to Speed 2 and add eggs, one at a time, beating 30 seconds after each addition. Add ground sole, pepper, salt, nutmeg, parsley, and cream. Turn to Speed 4 and beat 1 minute. Refrigerate mixture for 30 minutes.

Shape mixture into 12 ovals using two large serving spoons. Arrange ovals in a greased 12-inch skillet. Carefully add lemon juice and boiling water into side of pan until quenelles are immersed. Simmer 15 minutes over medium heat. Drain well and serve immediately with *Caper Cheese Sauce.*

Yield: 5 to 6 servings.

Caper Cheese Sauce

---

2 tablespoons butter or margarine
3 tablespoons all-purpose flour
¾ cup milk
1 cup shredded Swiss cheese
1 tablespoon chopped capers
¼ teaspoon tarragon
1 tablespoon chopped parsley
¼ teaspoon salt
⅛ teaspoon pepper
½ cup heavy cream
1 tablespoon dry vermouth

Melt butter in saucepan over medium heat. Add flour and cook 2 minutes, stirring constantly. Gradually add milk, stirring until thickened. Add cheese, capers, tarragon, parsley, salt, pepper, cream, and vermouth. Cook and stir over low heat until cheese melts.

Yield: 1½ cups.

Stuffed Breast of Veal

One way to enjoy the special flavor of veal without the usual expense.

½ pound cooked ham,
  cut into 1-inch strips
3 slices bacon
1 medium onion,
  quartered
2 cloves garlic
3 tablespoons olive oil
⅓ cup parsley
2 teaspoons basil
3 slices white bread
2 packages (10 oz. each)
  frozen chopped
  spinach, thawed
¾ cup Parmesan cheese
1 egg
¼ teaspoon salt
¼ teaspoon pepper
1 (4 to 4½ pound) veal
  breast with pocket
¼ teaspoon thyme
1 cup dry white wine

Assemble and attach Food Grinder with coarse grinding plate. Turn to Speed 4 and grind ham, bacon, onion, and garlic. Heat 1 tablespoon olive oil in a 12-inch skillet. Add ground mixture and sauté 4 minutes. Add parsley and basil and cook 3 minutes longer. Remove from heat and set aside.

Wring spinach in a towel until very dry. Assemble and attach clean Food Grinder with coarse grinding plate. Turn to Speed 4 and grind spinach and bread into bowl. Add ham mixture, Parmesan cheese, egg, salt, and pepper. Attach bowl and flat beater. Turn to Stir Speed and mix 30 seconds.

Stuff pocket in veal breast with ham/spinach mixture. Secure pocket with string or skewers. Rub meat with remaining olive oil and sprinkle with remaining basil and thyme.

Brown stuffed breast in a large oven-proof pot over medium heat. Add wine and bring to a boil. Cover and bake at 375°F for 2 to 2½ hours, or until meat is tender at the pricking of a fork.

Transfer meat to a cutting board, rib bones facing up. Remove string or skewers. With a sharp knife, work the ends of the ribs loose and discard them. Put the meat on a warm serving platter, skin side up, and carve into thin slices, cutting on a slant toward the backbone. Serve immediately.

Yield: 4 to 6 servings.

Sauerbraten

1 onion, halved
2 stalks celery
2 carrots, peeled
1 cup dry red wine
1 cup red wine vinegar
1 teaspoon salt
2 bay leaves, crushed
1 teaspoon sage
1 teaspoon rosemary
3 cloves garlic, minced
1 tablespoon black
  peppercorns
2 tablespoons chopped
  parsley
1 (5 pound) rump roast
¼ cup vegetable oil
2 cups beef broth
3 tablespoons
  cornstarch

Assemble and attach Rotor Slicer/Shredder using thin slicer cone (No. 4). Turn to Speed 4 and slice onion, celery, and carrots. Add wine, vinegar, salt, bay leaves, sage, rosemary, garlic, peppercorns, and parsley to vegetables and mix well. Pour mixture over meat in a large glass bowl. Cover and refrigerate 24 hours, turning meat occasionally.

Remove meat from marinade and wipe dry. Strain marinade, discarding vegetables and spices; set aside. Heat oil in a large Dutch oven over medium heat. Add meat and brown on all sides. Add 1 cup beef broth and simmer, covered, over medium heat for 2 hours, turning occasionally.

Mix remaining broth with reserved marinade. Add to meat and cook 3 hours longer.

When meat is done, remove to a large platter. Strain cooking liquid into a medium saucepan and bring to a boil over medium heat. Blend cornstarch with 4 tablespoons of liquid and add to saucepan. Cook, stirring occasionally, until slightly thickened. Serve immediately with roast.

Yield: 8 servings.

Cornish Hens with Wild Rice Stuffing

The surprise is in the stuffing.

2 tablespoons butter or margarine
2 stalks celery, cut into ½-inch pieces
¾ cup dried apricots
2 cups cooked wild and white rice
½ teaspoon salt
⅛ teaspoon allspice
4 Cornish game hens
8 slices bacon

Heat butter in skillet over medium heat. Add celery and sauté 2 minutes. Remove celery from pan and set aside.

Assemble and attach Food Grinder using coarse grinding plate. Turn to Speed 4 and grind celery and apricots into a bowl. Add butter from sauté pan, rice, salt, and allspice; mix well.

Stuff each hen with mixture. Truss hens and crisscross 2 strips of bacon over each hen. Place on rack in baking pan and bake at 350°F for 1½ to 2 hours. Serve immediately.

Yield: 4 servings.

Beef and Snow Peas

1 large onion, halved
¼ pound mushrooms
3 tablespoons peanut oil
2 cloves garlic, minced
1 pound sirloin, thinly sliced
2 tablespoons sherry
1 package (6 oz.) frozen snow peas, thawed
¾ cup beef broth
2 tablespoons cornstarch
2 tablespoons soy sauce
¾ teaspoon salt
⅛ teaspoon pepper
¼ teaspoon ground ginger
Hot cooked rice

Assemble and attach Rotor Slicer/Shredder using thick slicer cone (No. 3). Turn to Speed 4 and slice onion and mushrooms, keeping each separate.

Heat 1 tablespoon oil in a 12-inch skillet or wok over medium heat. Add garlic and meat. Stir-fry 3 minutes or until meat is cooked. Remove from pan and set aside.

Heat remaining oil in pan. Add onion and stir-fry 1 minute. Add sherry and cook 30 seconds. Add pea pods and stir-fry 1 minute. Add mushrooms and stir-fry 1 minute more.

Return beef to pan. Mix beef broth, cornstarch, soy sauce, salt, pepper, and ground ginger together. Add to pan and cook, stirring occasionally, until thickened. Serve immediately over hot cooked rice.

Yield: 4 to 6 servings.

Mild Breakfast Sausage

3 pounds pork shoulder
    cut into 1-inch strips
¼ cup minced onion
4 teaspoons sage
½ teaspoon savory
3 teaspoons salt
1 teaspoon pepper
1 cup chopped parsley
½ teaspoon chervil
⅛ teaspoon marjoram
    Dash allspice
2 tablespoons water
1 egg, beaten
1 tablespoon shortening
    Natural or synthetic
    casings

Place pork on a metal baking sheet and freeze 20 minutes. Combine onion, sage, savory, salt, pepper, parsley, chervil, marjoram, and allspice. Sprinkle mixture over pork. Assemble and attach Food Grinder using coarse grinding plate. Turn to Speed 4 and grind pork into bowl. Add water and egg. Attach bowl and flat beater. Turn to Stir Speed and mix 1 minute.

Remove knife and coarse grinding plate from Food Grinder. Assemble and attach Sausage Stuffer. Grease Stuffer with shortening and slide casing on tightly. Tie off end of casing. Turn to Speed 4 and stuff pork mixture into casings. Twist sausage into smaller links and refrigerate or freeze until ready to use.

Yield: 3 pounds sausage.

Use natural or synthetic casings to stuff sausage; they can usually be found at your local butcher. Soak natural casings before using in cold water for 30 minutes to remove excess salt; then rinse several times by running cold water through the entire length of casing.

Pack the Sausage Stuffer with 3 to 4 feet of casings. Depending on the amount of meat ground for a recipe, it may be necessary to repack it several times.

Avoid packing meat mixture into casing too tightly; allow room for twisting sausage into links and for expansion during cooking.

If air bubbles develop, prick with a toothpick or skewer.

Moussaka

Our adaptation of the traditional Greek dish, this recipe is well worth
the preparation time and guaranteed to bring raves from your guests.

3 medium eggplants,
sliced ¼-inch thick

½ cup water

3 medium onions, cut
into sixths

2 cloves garlic

2 pounds boneless
lamb, cut into 1-inch
cubes

2 tablespoons olive oil

1 can (8 oz.) tomato
sauce

6 tablespoons tomato
paste

1 tablespoon sugar

½ cup dry red wine

½ teaspoon cinnamon

½ teaspoon nutmeg

1 bay leaf

½ teaspoon basil

½ teaspoon salt

¼ teaspoon pepper

8 tablespoons butter

6 tablespoons all-
purpose flour

4 cups milk

4 eggs, beaten

½ cup bread crumbs

1¾ cups Parmesan cheese

Arrange eggplant in a 9 x 13 x 2-inch pan and sprinkle
with water. Cover tightly and bake at 400°F for
30 minutes. Drain on paper towels and set aside.

Assemble and attach Food Grinder using fine grinding
plate. Turn to Speed 4 and grind onions, garlic, and lamb.
Heat oil in a 12-inch skillet over medium heat. Add
ground mixture and cook until browned; drain well. Add
tomato sauce, tomato paste, sugar, red wine, cinnamon,
nutmeg, bay leaf, basil, salt, and pepper; mix well.
Reduce heat and simmer 30 minutes. Remove bay leaf.

Melt butter in a large saucepan over medium heat. Add
flour and stir until smooth. Gradually add milk, stirring
constantly, and cook until mixture thickens. Add eggs,
bread crumbs, and 1½ cups Parmesan cheese. Remove
from heat and set aside.

Arrange half of eggplant slices in a greased 9 x 13 x 2-inch
pan. Top with meat mixture. Sprinkle remaining ¼ cup
Parmesan cheese over meat mixture and top with
remaining eggplant. Spread milk mixture over eggplant.
Bake at 350°F for 50 to 60 minutes or until top is brown.
Cool 15 minutes before serving.

Yield: 8 servings.

Chicken Croquettes

Don't wait for leftovers to serve this dish.

2 tablespoons butter or margarine
½ cup all-purpose flour
Dash nutmeg
½ cup milk
2½ cups cooked chicken
1 teaspoon lemon juice
½ teaspoon salt
¼ teaspoon pepper
¼ teaspoon sage
2 tablespoons chopped parsley
1 tablespoon minced onion
2 tablespoons chicken broth
2 eggs, beaten
½ cup bread crumbs
Vegetable oil for frying

Melt butter in a small saucepan over medium heat. Add 2 tablespoons flour and nutmeg and cook 2 minutes. Gradually add milk, stirring constantly, until mixture starts to thicken. Cook 2 minutes longer. Remove from heat and set aside.

Assemble and attach Food Grinder using coarse grinding plate. Turn to Speed 4 and grind chicken into bowl. Add milk mixture, lemon juice, salt, pepper, sage, parsley, onion, and chicken broth. Attach bowl and flat beater. Turn to Speed 2 and mix 1 minute. Shape mixture into 8 cones. Refrigerate 15 minutes.

Coat each croquette with remaining flour, then egg, then bread crumbs. Heat 1-inch of oil to 365°F in a 12-inch skillet over medium-high heat. Fry croquettes 3 minutes on each side or until golden brown. Drain on paper towels. Serve immediately with *Chicken Cream Sauce.*

Yield: 4 servings.

Chicken Cream Sauce

2 tablespoons butter or margarine
2 tablespoons all-purpose flour
¾ cup chicken broth
¼ cup heavy cream

Melt butter in a small saucepan over medium heat. Add flour and cook 1 minute. Gradually add chicken broth and stir until mixture is smooth and thick. Cook 2 minutes longer, stirring occasionally. Stir in heavy cream.

Yield: 1 cup.

Shrimp Gumbo

1 medium onion,
  halved

1 large green pepper,
  seeded and quartered

3 stalks celery

4 tablespoons olive oil

2 cloves garlic, minced

1 can (28 oz.) whole
  tomatoes, coarsely
  chopped

2 cans (8 oz.) tomato
  sauce

1 teaspoon sugar

½ teaspoon salt

1 bay leaf

1 teaspoon thyme

1 tablespoon chopped
  parsley

1 teaspoon hot pepper
  sauce

2 pounds medium
  shrimp, shelled and
  deveined

  Hot cooked rice

Assemble and attach Rotor Slicer/Shredder using thick slicer cone (No. 3). Turn to Speed 4 and slice onion, green pepper, and celery, keeping each separate.

Heat oil in a 5-quart pot over medium heat. Add garlic and sauté 1 minute. Add onion and sauté 2 minutes. Add green pepper and celery and sauté 3 minutes more.

Add tomatoes, tomato sauce, sugar, salt, bay leaf, thyme, parsley, and hot pepper sauce. Reduce heat and simmer 15 minutes. Add shrimp; stir gently and cook 4 to 5 minutes longer. Serve immediately over hot cooked rice.

Yield: 6 servings.

Chicken Kiev

Chicken breasts rolled around a delicate filling of butter and herbs.

4 whole chicken
  breasts, boned,
  skinned and split
½ cup butter or
  margarine, softened
1 tablespoon chopped
  shallots
1 teaspoon minced
  garlic
1 teaspoon tarragon
¼ teaspoon pepper
¼ teaspoon salt
1 teaspoon lemon juice
1 tablespoon chopped
  parsley
6 slices white bread
½ cup all-purpose flour
2 eggs, beaten
  Vegetable oil for
  frying

Pound chicken between waxed paper until thin. Refrigerate until needed. Place butter, shallots, garlic, tarragon, pepper, salt, lemon juice, and parsley in bowl. Attach bowl and flat beater. Turn to Speed 2 and mix 30 seconds. Set aside.

Assemble and attach Food Grinder using fine grinding plate. Turn to Speed 4 and grind bread.

Place 1 tablespoon butter-herb mixture in center of each piece of chicken. Roll and secure with toothpicks. Coat each roll with flour, then dip in egg and coat with fresh bread crumbs. Chill chicken at least 2 hours.

Heat 1 inch of oil to 365°F in a 4-quart saucepan over medium heat. Fry rolls for 3 to 4 minutes on each side or until golden brown. Drain on paper towels. Serve immediately.

Yield: 4 servings.

Osso Buco

"Bone with a Hole"—classic Italian dish of veal shanks slowly braised
with vegetables and herbs until tender.

1 large onion, cut into
sixths

2 carrots, peeled and
cut into 1-inch pieces

2 stalks celery, cut into
1-inch pieces

2 cloves garlic

¼ cup butter or
margarine

1 tablespoon lemon
peel

1 cup all-purpose flour

¼ teaspoon salt

⅛ teaspoon pepper

½ cup olive oil

6 pounds veal shanks,
cut into 2½-inch
lengths

1 cup dry white wine

2 cans (28 oz. each)
Italian tomatoes,
seeded and coarsely
chopped with juice
reserved

½ teaspoon basil

¼ teaspoon thyme

2 bay leaves

3 sprigs parsley

Assemble and attach Food Grinder using coarse grinding
plate. Turn to Speed 4 and grind onion, carrot, celery, and
garlic. Melt butter in a large Dutch oven or roaster over
medium heat. Add ground vegetables and sauté 5 minutes,
or until tender. Remove from heat and stir in lemon
peel.

Combine flour, salt, and pepper; dredge meat in flour
mixture. Heat half of oil in a 12-inch skillet. Brown half
of meat until golden brown. Add remaining oil and brown
remaining meat. Place meat, cut side up, on vegetables
in Dutch oven.

Drain fat from skillet and add wine. Boil 1 to 2 minutes,
scraping up the cooking residues from the bottom of the
pan. Pour mixture over meat.

Combine tomatoes and reserved juice, basil, thyme, bay
leaves, and parsley. Pour over meat and bring mixture to
a simmer over medium heat. Bake in lower third of oven
at 350°F for 1½ to 2 hours, or until meat is tender.

Yield: 6 to 8 servings.

Scallops Provençale

Fresh scallops and mushrooms simmered in a light but spicy tomato sauce.

¼ pound fresh
  mushrooms
1 can (28 oz.) Italian
  tomatoes, seeded,
  juice reserved
1 tablespoon olive oil
1 tablespoon butter or
  margarine
4 cloves garlic, minced
1 pound bay or sea
  scallops
2 tablespoons red wine
2 tablespoons chopped
  parsley
1 tablespoon lemon
  juice
¼ teaspoon oregano
¼ teaspoon basil
  Salt and pepper
  Hot cooked rice

Assemble and attach Rotor Slicer/Shredder using thick slicer cone (No. 3). Turn to Speed 4 and slice mushrooms; set aside. Turn to Speed 4 and coarsely chop tomatoes.

Heat butter and olive oil in a 12-inch skillet over medium heat. Add garlic and sauté 1 minute. Add scallops and sauté 1 minute. Add mushrooms and cook another minute.

Add tomatoes and their juice, red wine, parsley, lemon juice, oregano, basil, salt, and pepper; stir well. Reduce heat and simmer 5 to 7 minutes. Serve immediately with hot cooked rice.

Yield: 4 servings.

When selecting scallops, choose ones that are translucent and shiny in appearance and have a sweetish aroma.

Pork Goulash

Pork, sauerkraut and potatoes simmered slow and long until fork tender.

2 onions, quartered

4 tomatoes, peeled, halved and seeded

2 pounds pork loin, cut into 1-inch cubes

¼ cup all-purpose flour

2 tablespoons vegetable oil

1 clove garlic, minced

3 tablespoons tomato paste

2 tablespoons chopped parsley

1 bay leaf

¼ teaspoon thyme

1 teaspoon salt

¼ teaspoon pepper

1 cup dry white wine

1 cup water

1 pound potatoes, peeled

¾ pound sauerkraut, rinsed and drained

2 tablespoons paprika

1½ teaspoons caraway seeds (optional)

Hot buttered noodles

Sour cream

Assemble and attach Rotor Slicer/Shredder using thick slicer cone (No. 3). Turn to Speed 4 and slice onions; set aside. Turn to Speed 4 and coarsely sliver tomatoes; set aside.

Dredge pork in flour. Heat oil in a 5-quart pot over medium-high heat. Add pork and cook until browned. Remove meat and set aside. Add onion and garlic to pot and sauté 2 minutes. Drain excess oil. Add tomatoes and cook 2 minutes more. Return pork to pot. Add tomato paste, parsley, bay leaf, thyme, salt, pepper, wine, and water. Bring mixture to a boil, then reduce heat and simmer 50 minutes.

Exchange thick slicer cone for coarse shredder cone (No. 2). Turn to Speed 4 and shred potatoes. Add potatoes, sauerkraut, paprika, and caraway seeds to pot. Cover and simmer 1 hour; add more water if necessary. Serve immediately over hot buttered noodles with sour cream.

Yield: 6 to 8 servings.

Mushroom Swiss Onion Quiche

½ pound Swiss cheese
1 small onion, halved
¼ pound fresh
    mushrooms
1 pre-baked 9-inch
    pastry shell
4 eggs
1 cup heavy cream
1 teaspoon salt
2 tablespoons parsley
    Dash hot pepper sauce
3 slices bacon, crisply
    cooked and crumbled

Assemble and attach Rotor Slicer/Shredder using fine shredder cone (No. 1). Turn to Speed 4 and shred cheese and onion, keeping each separate. Exchange fine shredder cone for thick slicer cone (No. 3). Turn to Speed 4 and slice mushrooms.

Place half of shredded cheese in pastry shell. Arrange sliced mushrooms on top of cheese. Arrange onion on top of mushrooms.

Place eggs in bowl. Attach bowl and flat beater. Turn to Speed 4 and beat 3 minutes. Add cream, salt, parsley, and hot pepper sauce. Turn to Speed 4 and beat 1 minute. Pour mixture into shell.

Top with remaining cheese and sprinkle with bacon. Bake at 350°F for 30 minutes. Knife inserted in center will come out clean when done. Serve immediately.

Yield: One 9-inch pie.

Italian Sausage

It's all in the herbs and spices and the freshly ground pork.

3 pounds pork shoulder,
    cut into 1-inch strips
3 teaspoons salt
1½ teaspoons pepper
1¼ teaspoons cayenne
    pepper
2 cloves garlic, minced
1 teaspoon onion
    powder
1 teaspoon paprika
⅛ teaspoon marjoram
⅛ teaspoon rosemary
⅛ teaspoon thyme
½ cup dry red wine
1 tablespoon shortening
    Natural or synthetic
    casings

Place pork on a metal baking sheet and freeze 20 minutes. Combine salt, pepper, cayenne pepper, garlic, onion powder, paprika, marjoram, rosemary, and thyme. Sprinkle mixture over pork. Assemble and attach Food Grinder using coarse grinding plate. Turn to Speed 4 and grind pork into bowl. Add wine. Attach bowl and flat beater. Turn to Stir Speed and mix 1 minute.

Remove knife and coarse grinding plate from Food Grinder. Assemble and attach Sausage Stuffer. Grease Stuffer with shortening and slide casing on tightly. Tie off end of casing. Turn to Speed 4 and stuff pork mixture into casings. Twist sausage into smaller links and refrigerate or freeze until ready to use.

Yield: 3 pounds sausage.

Pork Chops with Sweet Potatoes and Apples

3 medium sweet
  potatoes, peeled
3 medium apples,
  peeled and cored
1 small onion
4 slices bacon
4 loin chops (1 inch
  thick), fat trimmed
1 tablespoon lemon
  juice
¼ teaspoon salt
⅛ teaspoon pepper
⅛ teaspoon nutmeg
¼ teaspoon chervil
1 tablespoon chopped
  parsley

Assemble and attach Rotor Slicer/Shredder using coarse shredder cone (No. 2). Turn to Speed 4 and shred sweet potatoes, apples, and onion.

Cook bacon in 12-inch skillet over medium-high heat until crisp. Drain all but 1 tablespoon fat. Crumble bacon and set aside.

Rub pork chops with lemon juice; brown in bacon fat. Remove from pan and set aside. Drain all but 1 tablespoon fat. Add sweet potatoes, apples, and onion to pan. Cook 5 minutes, stirring occasionally. Add salt, pepper, nutmeg, and chervil; mix well.

Place vegetable mixture in a greased 9 x 9 x 2-inch pan. Arrange pork chops on top of mixture and sprinkle with chopped parsley. Cover tightly and bake at 350°F for 50 to 60 minutes, or until pork chops are tender. Serve immediately.

Yield: 4 servings.

Beef Roulade

Seasoned ground beef with a delicious spinach filling,
this recipe is ideally suited to your next buffet.

1½ pounds ground beef
1½ cups fresh bread
  crumbs
  2 eggs
¾ cup milk
½ cup catsup
¼ cup Parmesan cheese
¼ cup chopped parsley
1½ teaspoons oregano
⅛ teaspoon garlic
  powder
½ teaspoon salt
¼ teaspoon pepper
2 packages (10 oz. each)
  frozen, chopped
  spinach, thawed
1 cup ricotta cheese

Place ground beef, bread crumbs, eggs, milk, catsup, Parmesan cheese, parsley, oregano, garlic powder, salt, and pepper in bowl. Attach bowl and flat beater. Turn to Speed 2 and mix for 1 minute. Turn out onto waxed paper, and shape into a 10 x 14-inch rectangle.

Place spinach in a towel and wring until very dry. Place spinach and ricotta cheese in bowl. Attach bowl and flat beater. Turn to Speed 2 and mix for 1 minute. Spread spinach mixture on top of meat mixture. Roll up, beginning at longest side. Press edges and ends of roll together to seal.

Place on greased baking sheet, seam side down. Bake at 350°F for 1 hour. Serve immediately.

Yield: Fourteen 1-inch servings.

Steamed Mussels with Herbs

One of life's simple dishes. Serve with lots of crusty bread
to soak up the broth.

2 stalks celery
2 small onions, halved
¼ cup butter or
   margarine
1 clove garlic, minced
2 tablespoons chopped
   parsley
1 bay leaf
½ teaspoon thyme
¼ teaspoon basil
¼ teaspoon pepper
½ teaspoon salt
¼ cup dry white wine
2 tablespoons lemon
   juice
2 quarts mussels,
   cleaned

Assemble and attach Rotor Slicer/Shredder using thin
slicer cone (No. 4). Turn to Speed 4 and slice celery and
onions.

Melt butter over medium heat in a 5-quart pot. Add
celery and onions and sauté 1 minute. Add garlic, parsley,
bay leaf, thyme, basil, pepper, salt, wine, and lemon
juice; stir well.

Bring mixture to a boil and add mussels. Cover pot and
simmer 7 to 10 minutes. Drain mussels, reserving broth.
Strain broth through cheesecloth and pour over mussels.
Serve immediately.

Yield: 4 servings.

To clean mussels: Scrub mussels well in several changes of water,
scraping off beards. Let mussels soak in cold water sprinkled with a
handful of cornmeal for 1 hour to remove any sand; or soak them in
clear, cold water for several hours or overnight. Then drain and give
mussels a final rinse under cold running water.

Beef Stroganoff

1 pound sirloin, thinly sliced

3 tablespoons olive oil

3 tablespoons red wine vinegar

1 large onion, quartered

½ pound fresh mushrooms

¼ cup butter or margarine

1 teaspoon salt

¼ teaspoon pepper

½ cup dry white wine

1 cup sour cream

¼ teaspoon Dijon-style mustard

1 tablespoon Worcestershire sauce

Hot buttered noodles

Place meat, oil, and vinegar in a glass bowl; mix well. Cover and refrigerate 2 hours. Drain beef and dry with paper towel.

Assemble and attach Rotor Slicer/Shredder using thick slicer cone (No. 3). Turn to Speed 4 and slice onion and mushrooms; set aside.

Melt butter in a 12-inch skillet over medium-high heat. Add meat and sauté until just barely cooked. Remove from pan and set aside. Add onion and mushrooms to pan and sauté 1 minute. Reduce heat and add salt, pepper, and wine. Cook 5 minutes. Return beef to pan and cook 1 minute. Remove from heat and stir in sour cream, mustard, and Worcestershire sauce. Serve immediately over hot buttered noodles.

Yield: 6 servings.

It is easier to slice beef and pork when they are partially frozen.

The perfect mixer!

Who can resist the temptation of this simple food, particularly when it's homemade. With the help of your KitchenAid Pasta Maker, this fabulous taste sensation can be yours just for the making. Nutritious and inexpensive, it offers almost as many variations in flavors as in shapes. It can launch a meal, be the accompaniment to a main dish, or serve as the main course itself. Choose from a repertoire of first-rate recipes guaranteed to fire up your taste buds.

Basic Egg Noodle Pasta

4 large eggs (⅞ cup eggs)
1 tablespoon water
3½ cups **sifted** all-purpose
  flour

Place eggs, water, and flour in bowl. Attach bowl and flat beater. Turn to Speed 2 and mix for 30 seconds.

Remove flat beater and attach dough hook. Turn to Speed 2 and knead 2 minutes.

Hand knead dough for 30 seconds to 1 minute. Cover with dry towel and let rest 15 minutes before extruding through Pasta Maker.

Follow cooking instructions "To Cook Pasta," page 86.

Yield: 1¼ pounds dough.

Whole Wheat Pasta

4 large eggs (⅞ cup eggs)
2 tablespoons water
3½ cups **sifted** whole
  wheat flour

Place eggs, water, and flour in bowl. Attach bowl and flat beater. Turn to Speed 2 and mix 30 seconds.

Remove flat beater and attach dough hook. Turn to Speed 2 and knead 1 minute.

Hand knead dough for 30 seconds to 1 minute. Cover with dry towel and let rest 15 minutes before extruding through Pasta Maker.

Follow cooking instructions "To Cook Pasta," page 86.

Yield: 1¼ pounds dough.

Always *sift* flour directly into measuring cup before adding to bowl.

High humidity can cause pasta dough to become sticky and difficult to extrude. To avoid this problem, prepare dough using only the *sifted* flour and eggs. Stop and check consistency. If dough is too dry, add the water, a teaspoon at a time, and remix using flat beater; or knead dough with wet hands.

Spinach Pasta

1 package (10 oz.)
  frozen, chopped
  spinach, thawed
1 tablespoon water
4 large eggs (⅞ cup
  eggs)
4 cups **sifted** all-
  purpose flour

Place spinach in a towel and wring out all water until spinach feels very dry. Assemble and attach Food Grinder using fine grinding plate. Turn to Speed 4 and grind spinach. Discard unground spinach that remains in grinder body.

Place ground spinach, water, and eggs in bowl. Attach bowl and flat beater. Turn to Speed 4 and mix 30 seconds. Add flour to bowl. Turn to Speed 2 and mix 45 seconds.

Remove flat beater and attach dough hook. Turn to Speed 2 and knead 1 minute.

Hand knead dough for 30 seconds to 1 minute. Cover with dry towel and let rest 15 minutes before extruding through Pasta Maker.

Follow cooking instructions "To Cook Pasta," page 86.

Yield: 1½ pounds dough.

NOTE: For best results use only Flat Noodle (Plate 3), Macaroni (Plate 4), and Lasagna (Plate 5) plates with this recipe.

Pasta Alla Carbonara
Richly flavored Italian specialty of pasta with bacon, cream and peas.

¼ pound bacon cut into
  ½-inch pieces
½ cup chopped onion
½ package (10 oz.)
  frozen green peas,
  thawed
1½ cups heavy cream
1 cup grated Parmesan
  cheese
  Salt and pepper
1 pasta recipe or 1½
  pounds of flat
  noodles or spaghetti,
  cooked and drained

Cook bacon in a 12-inch skillet over medium-high heat until crisp. Remove from pan and pour off all but 1 tablespoon fat. Add onion and sauté 3 minutes. Add peas and sauté 3 minutes more. Stir in reserved bacon, heavy cream, Parmesan cheese, salt, and pepper. Heat through but do not boil. Serve immediately over hot pasta.

Yield: 3 cups.

Chinese Noodles

A hot and tangy orientation for plain old pasta.

½ cup peanut oil

2 tablespoons rice vinegar or white wine vinegar

1 tablespoon dry sherry

2½ tablespoons sesame oil

3 tablespoons soy sauce

1 tablespoon crushed red pepper

½ teaspoon ground ginger

1 tablespoon brown sugar

1 tablespoon chopped onion

¼ cup diced green pepper

1 pasta recipe or 1½ pounds of spaghetti, cooked and drained

Combine all ingredients. Toss well and refrigerate 2 hours, stirring occasionally.

Yield: 8 servings.

Spinach Pasta Pomodoro

Nutritious spinach pasta with a light tomato sauce; a superb side dish.

5 large tomatoes, cut
  into sixths
3 tablespoons olive oil
3 cloves garlic, minced
½ cup chopped fresh
  basil
1 teaspoon sugar
1 teaspoon salt
¼ teaspoon pepper
  Parmesan cheese
1 pasta recipe or 1½
  pounds of spinach
  flat noodles, cooked
  and drained

Assemble and attach Fruit/Vegetable Strainer. Turn to Speed 4 and strain tomatoes. Measure out 3 cups puree and set aside.

Heat oil in a 2-quart saucepan over medium heat. Add garlic and sauté 2 minutes. Add tomato puree, basil, sugar, salt, and pepper. Reduce heat; cover and simmer for 30 minutes. Serve immediately over hot pasta with Parmesan cheese.

Yield: 3 cups.

Chicken Noodle Amandine

Mushrooms and chicken provide the flavor; orange the zest; almonds the crunch; and sour cream the final touch.

1 cup slivered almonds
½ cup butter or
  margarine
2 cups mushrooms,
  sliced
2 tablespoons grated
  orange peel
3 teaspoons salt
¼ teaspoon pepper
½ cup chicken broth
4 cups cooked chicken,
  cut into cubes
3 cups sour cream
1 pasta recipe or 1½
  pounds of flat noodles,
  cooked and drained

Melt ¼ cup butter in a saucepan over medium heat. Add almonds and stir until lightly browned. Remove from heat and set aside.

Melt remaining butter in a clean saucepan over medium heat. Add mushrooms and sauté for 3 minutes. Add orange peel, salt, pepper, broth, and chicken pieces. Continue cooking an additional minute. Stir sour cream into chicken mixture, heat through, but do not boil. Serve immediately over hot noodles. Sprinkle with almonds.

Yield: 6 to 8 servings.

Pasta Con Salsice

An all-time favorite of fresh pasta with sausage, green pepper and onion.

1 ½ pounds boneless pork
    shoulder cut into
    1-inch strips
2 cloves garlic
1 ½ tablespoons chopped
    parsley
¾ tablespoon crushed
    red pepper
1 tablespoon fennel
    seed
2 teaspoons salt
½ cup dry red wine
1 tablespoon shortening
    Natural or synthetic
    sausage casings
3 tablespoons olive oil
3 medium green
    peppers, seeded,
    halved and sliced
3 medium onions,
    halved and sliced
1 large clove garlic,
    minced
2 tablespoons chopped
    fresh basil
1 pasta recipe or 1 ½
    pounds of spaghetti,
    cooked and drained

Assemble and attach Food Grinder using coarse grinding plate. Turn to Speed 4 and grind pork and 2 cloves garlic. Add parsley, red pepper, fennel seed, 1 ½ teaspoons salt, and ¼ cup wine; mix well.

Remove coarse grinding plate and knife from Food Grinder. Assemble and attach Sausage Stuffer. Grease Stuffer with shortening and slide casing on tightly. Tie off end of casing. Turn to Speed 4 and stuff pork mixture into casings. Twist sausage into 12 links and set aside.

Heat 1 tablespoon oil in a 12-inch skillet over medium heat. Add green pepper, onion, and garlic and sauté 5 minutes. Add remaining salt, wine, olive oil, and basil. Cook, stirring frequently, for 3 minutes. Remove from pan and set aside.

Add sausages to pan and cook until done; drain fat. Add pepper and onion mixture to cooked sausages and stir gently. Serve immediately over hot pasta.

Yield: 6 servings.

NOTE: Omit crushed red pepper to make mild sausage.

Shrimp and Feta Alla Grecque

An unusual blend of fresh shrimp, pungent feta cheese and scallions in a tomato-dill sauce. A dish that becomes more addictive with every bite.

1 pound medium shrimp, cleaned and cooked

1 pound feta cheese, drained and coarsely crumbled

1 cup sliced scallions

1 cup tomato sauce

½ cup olive oil

¼ cup fresh lemon juice

1 tablespoon chopped parsley

1 tablespoon chopped fresh basil

1 tablespoon chopped fresh dill

½ teaspoon salt

¼ teaspoon pepper

1 pasta recipe or 1½ pounds of flat noodles, cooked and drained

Combine shrimp, feta cheese, and scallions in a large bowl. Add tomato sauce, olive oil, lemon juice, parsley, basil, dill, salt, and pepper; mix well. Cover and refrigerate 1 hour.

Toss shrimp mixture with hot noodles and serve immediately or refrigerate 1 hour and serve cold.

Yield: 6 servings.

96

Pecan Rolls

Dynamite!

½ cup milk
¾ cup butter or
  margarine
¼ cup sugar
1 teaspoon salt
¼ cup warm water
  (105°F to 115°F)
1 package active dry
  yeast
3-3½ cups all-purpose flour
1 egg
1¼ cups brown sugar
¾ cup chopped pecans

Scald milk; stir in ¼ cup butter, sugar, and salt. Cool to lukewarm. Dissolve yeast in warm water in warmed bowl. Add lukewarm milk mixture, 2½ cups flour, and egg.

Attach bowl and dough hook. Turn to Speed 2 and mix 2 minutes, until well blended. Continuing on Speed 2, add remaining flour, ½ cup at a time, until dough clings to hook and cleans sides of bowl. Knead on Speed 2 for 3 to 5 minutes or until dough is smooth and elastic.

Place in a greased bowl, turning to grease top. Cover; let rise in warm place, free from draft, until doubled in bulk, about 45 minutes.

Punch dough down. Roll dough to a 12-inch square. Combine ½ cup brown sugar and ¼ cup pecans; sprinkle over dough. Roll dough tightly, pinching seams together. Cut into twelve 1-inch slices.

Melt remaining butter and add remaining brown sugar and pecans; mix well. Spoon into 12 greased muffin cups. Place one dough slice, cut side up, into each muffin cup. Cover; let rise in warm place, free from draft, until doubled in bulk, about 1 hour.

Bake at 350°F for 25 to 30 minutes. Invert pan on wire rack. Let stand 3 minutes, then remove.

Yield: 12 rolls.

Anadama Bread
Cornmeal and molasses flavor this New England bread.

2 cups cold water
1 cup cornmeal
½ cup molasses
⅓ cup butter or
   margarine
2 teaspoons salt
5-6 cups all-purpose flour
2 packages active dry
   yeast
2 eggs

Combine water and cornmeal in saucepan over medium heat. Cook and stir until thickened. Remove from heat and add molasses, butter, and salt; cool to lukewarm.

Place 4 cups flour and yeast in bowl. Attach bowl and dough hook. Turn to Speed 2 and mix 30 seconds. Gradually add cornmeal mixture and eggs and mix 2 minutes. Continuing on Speed 2, add remaining flour, ½ cup at a time, until dough clings to hook and cleans sides of bowl. Knead on Speed 2 for 3 to 5 minutes or until dough is smooth and elastic.

Place in a greased bowl, turning to grease top. Cover; let rise in warm place, free from draft, until doubled in bulk, about 1 hour.

Punch dough down and divide in half. Shape each half into a loaf and place in a greased 8½ x 4½ x 2½-inch loaf pan. Cover; let rise in warm place, free from draft, until *almost* doubled in bulk, about 45 minutes.

Bake at 375°F for 25 minutes. Cover loaves with aluminum foil and bake 15 minutes longer. Remove from pans immediately and cool on wire racks.

Yield: 2 loaves.

Apple Crumb Coffee Cake

½ cup milk
¼ cup butter or margarine
¼ cup warm water (105°F to 115°F)
3-3½ cups all-purpose flour
¼ cup sugar
1 teaspoon salt
1 package active dry yeast
1 egg
Cinnamon Crumb Filling
2 apples, peeled, cored and thinly sliced

Scald milk; add butter and water. Cool to lukewarm. Place 2 cups flour, sugar, salt, and yeast in bowl. Attach bowl and dough hook. Turn to Speed 2 and mix 30 seconds. Gradually add warm liquids to bowl, mixing 2 minutes. Add egg and mix 1 minute longer. Continuing on Speed 2, add remaining flour, ½ cup at a time, until dough clings to hook and cleans sides of bowl. Knead on Speed 2 for 5 to 7 minutes longer.

Place in a greased bowl, turning to grease top. Cover; let rise in warm place, free from draft, until doubled in bulk, about 1 hour.

Punch dough down and divide in half. Roll each half to a 9-inch circle. Place one circle in bottom of a greased 9-inch springform pan. Sprinkle ¼ of *Cinnamon Crumb Filling* over dough. Arrange half the apple slices on filling; sprinkle ¼ filling over apples. Place remaining dough circle in pan and repeat with remaining crumb mixture and apples. Cover; let rise in warm place, free from draft, until doubled in bulk, about 1 hour.

Bake at 375°F for 45 to 50 minutes. Remove sides of springform pan immediately and cool on wire rack.

Yield: 1 coffee cake.

Cinnamon Crumb Filling

1 cup sugar
¾ cup all-purpose flour
2½ teaspoons cinnamon
6 tablespoons butter or margarine, softened

Mix all ingredients with a fork until crumbly.

Dill Rye Bread

1¾ cups rye berries or 2
  cups rye flour
3¼-3¾ cups all-purpose
  flour
  2 tablespoons sugar
  2 teaspoons salt
  2 packages active dry
    yeast
  1 teaspoon caraway
    seed
  1 teaspoon dill seed
  ½ teaspoon dill weed
1¼ cups water
  ½ cup milk
  2 tablespoons butter or
    margarine
  1 egg white
  1 tablespoon cold water
  1 tablespoon sesame
    seed

Assemble and attach Grain Mill. Set Mill at Click 3.
Turn to Speed 10 and grind rye berries. Set flour aside.

Place 2 cups all-purpose flour, rye flour, sugar, salt, yeast,
caraway seed, dill seed, and dill weed in bowl. Attach bowl
and dough hook. Turn to Speed 2 and mix 30 seconds.

Combine water, milk, and butter in saucepan. Heat over
low heat until liquids are very warm (120°F to 130°F).
Turn to Speed 2 and gradually add warm liquids to flour
mixture, about 1 minute. Mix 3 minutes longer.
Continuing on Speed 2, add remaining flour, ½ cup at a
time, until dough clings to hook and cleans sides of
bowl. Knead on Speed 2 for 5 to 7 minutes longer.

Place in a greased bowl, turning to grease top. Cover; let
rise in warm place, free from draft, about 20 minutes.

Divide dough in half. Shape each half into a slightly
flattened ball and place on greased baking sheet. Cover;
let rise in warm place, free from draft, until doubled in
bulk, about 1 hour.

With a sharp knife make 4 slashes in tic-tac-toe pattern
on each loaf. Beat egg white and water together with a
fork. Brush each loaf with mixture and sprinkle with
sesame seed. Bake at 375°F for 30 to 35 minutes. Remove
from baking sheets immediately and cool on wire racks.

Yield: 2 loaves.

For an attractive thick crust, brush tops of loaves with beaten egg white
and water. For a softer crust with a rich golden color, brush with lightly
beaten whole egg; or one egg yolk, beaten with 1-2 tablespoons water or
milk, just before baking.

Three Grain Braid

Whole wheat, rye and white bread woven into a beautiful party loaf.

1¼ cups wheat berries or 1½ cups whole wheat flour

1¼ cups rye berries or 1½ cups rye flour

5-5¼ cups all-purpose flour

2 tablespoons sugar

1 tablespoon salt

2 packages active dry yeast ·

¼ cup butter or margarine, melted

2¼ cups warm water (105°F to 115°F)

4 tablespoons molasses

1 teaspoon caraway seed

1 tablespoon cocoa

Assemble and attach Grain Mill. Set Mill on Click 3. Turn to Speed 10 and grind wheat and rye berries, keeping each separate. Set flours aside.

Place 2½ cups all-purpose flour, sugar, salt, and yeast in bowl. Attach bowl and dough hook. Combine butter and water. Turn to Speed 2 and gradually add liquid to bowl, mixing until blended, about 2 minutes. Gradually add 1 cup all-purpose flour. Continuing on Speed 2, mix for 4 minutes. Remove ⅔ of batter from bowl and set aside.

Add 2 tablespoons molasses and whole wheat flour to ⅓ of batter in bowl. Turn to Speed 2 and knead 5 to 7 minutes, until dough clings to hook and cleans sides of bowl. Place dough in a greased bowl, cover, and set aside.

Place ⅓ batter, remaining molasses, caraway seed, cocoa, and rye flour in mixer bowl. Attach bowl and hook. Turn to Speed 2 and knead 5 to 7 minutes until dough clings to hook and cleans sides of bowl. Place dough in a greased bowl, cover, and set aside.

Place remaining ⅓ batter and 1½ cups all-purpose flour in mixer bowl. Attach bowl and hook. Turn to Speed 2 and knead 5 to 7 minutes, until dough clings to hook and cleans sides of bowl. Place dough in a greased bowl and cover.

Note: All three doughs may not form a ball on the hook; however, as long as there is contact between dough and hook, kneading will be accomplished. Do not add more than the maximum amount of flour specified or dry loaf will result.

Let doughs rise in warm place, free from draft, until doubled in bulk, about 1 hour. Punch doughs down; divide each in half. Roll each piece into a 15-inch rope. Braid a white, rye, and whole wheat rope together to form 1 loaf. Place on greased baking sheet. Repeat with remaining ropes. Cover; let rise in warm place, free from draft, until doubled in bulk, about 45 minutes.

Bake at 350°F for 30 to 40 minutes. Remove from baking sheets immediately and cool on wire racks.

Yield: 2 loaves.

Challah

This braided egg bread is traditionally served on the Jewish sabbath.

4½-5½ cups all-purpose flour

2 tablespoons sugar

1½ teaspoons salt

1 package active dry yeast

⅓ cup butter or margarine, melted

1 cup warm water (105°F to 115°F)

3 eggs

1 egg white

1 egg yolk

1 teaspoon cold water

1 teaspoon poppy seeds

Place 4 cups flour, sugar, salt, and yeast in bowl. Attach bowl and dough hook. Turn to Speed 2 and mix 30 seconds. Combine butter and water. Gradually add warm liquids to bowl and mix 2 minutes. Add eggs and egg white and mix 2 minutes more. Add remaining flour, ½ cup at a time, until dough clings to hook and cleans sides of bowl. Knead on Speed 2 for 7 to 10 minutes longer.

Place in a greased bowl, turning to grease top. Cover; let rise in warm place, free from draft, until doubled in bulk, about 1 hour.

Punch dough down and divide in half. Divide each half into three pieces. Roll each piece to a 14-inch rope. Braid three ropes together, tucking ends under, and place on greased baking sheet. Repeat with remaining ropes. Cover; let rise in warm place, free from draft, until doubled in bulk, about 1 hour.

Beat egg yolk and water together. Brush loaves with mixture and sprinkle with poppy seeds. Bake at 400°F for 30 to 35 minutes. Remove from baking sheets immediately and cool on wire racks.

Yield: 2 loaves.

Russian Black Bread

Hearty dark bread; the perfect accompaniment to your favorite winter soup.

1¾ cups rye berries or 2
   cups rye flour
1 cup water
2 tablespoons vinegar
2 tablespoons dark
   molasses
½ ounce (½ square)
   unsweetened
   chocolate
2 tablespoons butter or
   margarine
2 cups all-purpose flour
½ cup bran cereal
2 teaspoons caraway
   seed
½ teaspoon sugar
1 teaspoon salt
½ teaspoon instant
   coffee
½ teaspoon onion
   powder
1 package active dry
   yeast
½ teaspoon cornstarch

Assemble and attach Grain Mill. Set Mill on Click 3. Turn to Speed 10 and grind rye berries. Set flour aside.

Heat ¾ cup water, vinegar, molasses, and chocolate in small saucepan over medium heat until chocolate melts. Stir in butter and cool to lukewarm.

Mix flours together. Place 2½ cups flour mixture, cereal, caraway seed, sugar, salt, coffee, onion powder, and yeast in bowl. Attach bowl and dough hook. Turn to Speed 2 and mix 30 seconds. Continuing on Speed 2, gradually add warm liquids in a thin, steady stream, about 1 minute. Add remaining flour mixture, ½ cup at a time, until dough clings to hook and cleans sides of bowl. Knead on Speed 2 for 5 to 7 minutes or until smooth and elastic.

Note: Dough may not form a ball on the hook; however, as long as there is contact between dough and hook, kneading will be accomplished. Do not add more than the maximum amount of flour specified or dry loaf will result.

Place in a greased bowl, turning to grease top. Cover; let rise in warm place, free from draft, until doubled in bulk, about 1 hour.

Punch dough down and shape dough into a round loaf. Place in a greased 8-inch cake pan. Cover; let rise in warm place, free from draft, until doubled in bulk, about 1 hour.

Bake at 350°F for 35 to 40 minutes. Combine remaining water and cornstarch in small saucepan over medium heat. Stir constantly until mixture comes to a boil and cook for 30 seconds. Brush cornstarch mixture over loaf and return to oven for 2 minutes. Remove from pan immediately and cool on wire rack.

Yield: 1 loaf.

Cinnamon Pecan Coffee Cake

6½-7 cups all-purpose flour
½ cup sugar
1½ teaspoons salt
2 packages active dry yeast
1½ cups warm water (105°F to 115°F)
½ cup plus 2 tablespoons butter or margarine, melted
2 eggs
¾ cup chopped pecans
½ cup light brown sugar
1 teaspoon cinnamon

Place 4 cups flour, sugar, salt, and yeast in bowl. Attach bowl and dough hook. Turn to Speed 2 and mix 30 seconds. Combine water and ½ cup butter. Gradually add to bowl, mixing 3 minutes. Add eggs and mix 3 minutes longer. Continuing on Speed 2, add remaining flour, ½ cup at a time, until dough clings to hook and cleans sides of bowl. Knead on Speed 2 for 5 to 7 minutes longer.

Place in a greased bowl, turning to grease top. Cover with plastic wrap and refrigerate overnight.

Combine pecans, brown sugar, and cinnamon; set aside.

Punch dough down and divide in half. Roll one half to a 16 x 8 x ¼-inch rectangle. Brush with half the remaining butter and sprinkle with half the nut mixture. Roll dough tightly from 16-inch side, pinching seams to seal. Place on greased baking sheet, seam side down. Pinch ends together to form a ring. Cut ⅔ way into ring with scissors at 1-inch intervals. Turn each section on its side. Repeat with remaining dough. Cover; let rise in warm place, free from draft, until doubled in bulk, about 1 hour.

Bake at 375° for 25 to 30 minutes. Remove from baking sheets immediately and cool on wire racks.

Yield: 2 coffee cakes.

Potica

A delicious walnut-filled coffee cake

⅓ cup milk

¾ cup sugar

½ teaspoon salt

¼ cup plus 2 table-
spoons butter or
margarine

3 tablespoons warm
water (105°F to 115°F)

1 package active dry
yeast

3 eggs

2¾- 3½ cups all-purpose
flour

2 tablespoons heavy
cream

2 tablespoons honey

½ teaspoon cinnamon

1½ cups walnuts, ground
Powdered Sugar Icing

Scald milk; stir in ¼ cup sugar, salt, and ¼ cup butter. Cool to lukewarm.

Dissolve yeast in warm water in warmed bowl. Add lukewarm milk mixture, 2 eggs, and 2½ cups flour.

Attach bowl and dough hook. Turn to Speed 2 and mix 3 minutes. Continuing on Speed 2, add remaining flour, ¼ cup at a time, until dough clings to hook and cleans sides of bowl, about 3 minutes. Knead on Speed 2 for 5 to 7 minutes or until dough is smooth and elastic.

Place in a greased bowl, turning to grease top. Cover; let rise in warm place, free from draft, until doubled in bulk, about 1 hour.

Melt remaining butter in a 1-quart saucepan over medium heat. Add remaining sugar, cream, honey, and cinnamon; stir well. Bring to a full boil, and boil 30 seconds. Remove from heat and stir in walnuts. Cool slightly and stir in remaining egg. Set aside.

Punch dough down. Roll to a 12 x 14 x ¼-inch rectangle. Spread walnut mixture over dough. Roll dough tightly from longest side, pinching seam together to seal. Place seam side down on greased baking sheet; or coil loosely and place in greased oven-proof skillet.

Cover; let rise in warm place, free from draft, until doubled in bulk, about 45 minutes. Bake at 375°F for 25 to 30 minutes. Remove from pan immediately and cool on wire rack. When cool, drizzle with *Powdered Sugar Icing.*

Yield: 1 coffee cake.

Powdered Sugar Icing

---

1 cup powdered sugar

2-3 tablespoons milk

½ teaspoon vanilla

Combine all ingredients. Blend well to drizzling consistency.

Whole Grain Wheat Bread

You'll love this firm bread for sandwiches, toast—or fresh from the oven.

6-7 cups wheat berries or
   6-7 cups whole wheat
   flour
⅓ cup plus 1 tablespoon
   brown sugar
2¼ cups warm water
   (105°F to 115°F)
2 packages active dry
   yeast
¾ cup powdered milk
2 teaspoons salt
⅓ cup oil

Assemble and attach Grain Mill. Set Mill on Click 3. Turn to Speed 10 and grind wheat berries. Set aside.

Dissolve 1 tablespoon brown sugar in water and add yeast. Let mixture stand.

Place 5 cups flour, powdered milk, remaining brown sugar, and salt in bowl. Attach bowl and flat beater. Turn to Speed 2 and mix 1 minute. Continuing on Speed 2, gradually add yeast mixture and oil to flour mixture, about 2 to 3 minutes. Mix 1 minute longer.

Exchange beater for dough hook. Turn to Speed 2 and gradually add remaining flour, ½ cup at a time, until dough clings to hook and cleans sides of bowl. Knead on Speed 2 for 7 to 10 minutes longer.

Note: Dough may not form a ball on hook; however, as long as there is contact between dough and hook, kneading will be accomplished. Do not add more than the maximum amount of flour specified or dry loaf will result.

Place in a greased bowl, turning to grease top. Cover; let rise in a warm place, free from draft, until doubled in bulk, about 1 hour.

Punch dough down and divide in half. Shape each half into a loaf and place in a heavily greased 8½ x 4½ x 2½-inch loaf pan. Cover; let rise in warm place, free from draft, until doubled in bulk, about 1 hour. Bake at 400°F for 15 minutes, then reduce heat to 350°F and bake 25 minutes longer. Remove from pans immediately and cool on wire racks.

Yield: 2 loaves.

Herb Pull-Apart Rolls

Can also be seasoned with your own combination of herbs.

1 package active dry
yeast
1 cup warm water
(105°F to 115°F)
½ cup butter or
margarine, melted
3-3½ cups all-purpose flour
2 tablespoons sugar
1½ teaspoons salt
¼ teaspoon thyme
¼ teaspoon oregano
¼ teaspoon dill

Dissolve yeast in warm water in warmed bowl. Add ¼ cup butter, 2 cups flour, sugar, salt, thyme, oregano, and dill. Attach bowl and dough hook. Turn to Speed 2 and mix for 2 minutes, or until well blended. Continuing on Speed 2, add remaining flour, ½ cup at a time, until dough clings to hook and cleans sides of bowl. Knead on Speed 2 for 5 to 7 minutes longer, or until dough is smooth and elastic.

Place in a greased bowl, turning to grease top. Cover; let rise in warm place, free from draft, until doubled in bulk, about 1 hour.

Punch dough down. Roll dough to a 12 x 9 x ¼-inch rectangle. Brush with remaining butter. Slice dough into six 1½ x 12-inch strips. Stack strips, then cut into twelve 1-inch pieces. Place pieces, cut side up, in greased muffin cups. Cover; let rise in warm place, free from draft, until doubled in bulk, about 45 minutes.

Bake at 400°F for 15 to 20 minutes. Remove from pans immediately and cool on wire racks.

Yield: 1 dozen rolls.

Lemon Cheese Coffee Braid

⅓ cup milk

¾ cup sugar

½ teaspoon salt

¼ cup butter or margarine

3 tablespoons warm water (105°F to 115°F)

1 package active dry yeast

3 eggs

2¾-3½ cups all-purpose flour

2 packages (one 8 oz. and one 3 oz.) cream cheese, softened

1 teaspoon fresh grated lemon peel

½ cup raisins Powdered Sugar Icing

Scald milk; stir in ¼ cup sugar, salt, and butter. Cool to lukewarm.

Dissolve yeast in warm water in warmed bowl. Add lukewarm milk mixture, 2 eggs, and 2½ cups flour.

Attach bowl and dough hook. Turn to Speed 2 and mix 3 minutes. Continuing on Speed 2, add remaining flour, ¼ cup at a time, until dough clings to hook and cleans sides of bowl, about 3 minutes. Knead on Speed 2 for 5 to 7 minutes or until dough is smooth and elastic.

Place in a greased bowl, turning to grease top. Cover; let rise in warm place, free from draft, until doubled in bulk, about 1 hour.

Place cream cheese in clean bowl. Attach bowl and flat beater. Turn to Speed 4 and beat 1 minute. Stop and scrape bowl. Add remaining sugar and egg, and lemon peel. Turn to Speed 4 and beat 1 minute, until smooth. Reduce to Stir Speed and add raisins, mixing just until blended, about 15 seconds. Set mixture aside.

Punch dough down. Roll to a 12 x 14 x ¼-inch rectangle. Spread cream cheese mixture in a 4-inch strip down length of dough. Cut sides of dough into 1-inch strips almost to filling. Fold strips over filling, alternating from side to side.

Place on greased baking sheet. Cover; let rise in warm place, free from draft, until doubled in bulk, about 45 minutes.

Bake at 375°F for 25 to 30 minutes. Remove from baking sheet immediately and cool on wire rack. When cool, drizzle with *Powdered Sugar Icing*, page 106.

Yield: 1 coffee cake.

Honey-Oatmeal Bread

5-6 cups all-purpose flour
1 cup quick cooking oats
2 teaspoons salt
2 packages active dry yeast
1¾ cups water
½ cup honey
⅓ cup butter or margarine
2 eggs
1 tablespoon water
1 egg white
Oatmeal

Place 5 cups flour, oats, salt, and yeast in bowl. Attach bowl and dough hook. Turn to Speed 2 and mix for 30 seconds.

Combine water, honey, and butter in saucepan; heat to 120°F to 130°F. On Speed 2, slowly add warm liquids to flour mixture, about 1 minute. Add eggs and mix an additional minute.

Continuing on Speed 2, add remaining flour, ½ cup at a time, until dough clings to hook and cleans sides of bowl, about 3 minutes. Knead on Speed 2 for 7 to 10 minutes or until dough is smooth and elastic.

Place in a greased bowl, turning to grease top. Cover; let rise in warm place, free from draft, until doubled in bulk, about 1 hour.

Punch dough down. Divide dough in half. Shape each half into a loaf. Place each loaf in a greased 8½ x 4½ x 2½-inch loaf pan. Cover; let rise in warm place, free from draft, until doubled in bulk, about 1 hour.

Combine water and egg white. Brush tops of loaves with mixture. Sprinkle with oatmeal. Bake at 375°F for 40 minutes. Remove from pans immediately and cool on wire racks.

Yield: 2 loaves.

Clockwise: Three Grain Braid, Dill Rye Bread, Honey-Oatmeal Bread

Arab Bread

Sometimes called pita or pocket bread; just right for stuffing with sandwich filling or spicy Middle Eastern foods.

1¾ cups wheat berries or 2 cups whole wheat flour

3-3½ cups all-purpose flour

1 tablespoon sugar

2 teaspoons salt

1 package active dry yeast

2 cups warm water (120°F to 130°F)

Assemble and attach Grain Mill. Set Mill on Click 3. Turn to Speed 10 and grind berries. Set aside.

Mix flours together. Place 4 cups flour mixture, sugar, salt, and yeast in bowl. Attach bowl and dough hook. Turn to Speed 2 and mix 30 seconds. Gradually add warm water to bowl and mix 2 minutes. Continuing on Speed 2, add remaining flour mixture, ½ cup at a time, until dough clings to hook and cleans sides of bowl. Knead on Speed 2 for 5 to 7 minutes longer, or until dough is smooth and elastic.

Place in a greased bowl, turning to grease top. Cover; let rise in warm place, free from draft, until doubled in bulk, about 1 hour.

Punch dough down and divide into six equal pieces. Roll each piece into a 7-inch circle. Place circles on aluminum foil and let rise, uncovered, at room temperature for 1 hour.

Bake circles individually on foil at 500°F for 5 to 6 minutes. Remove from foil immediately and cool on wire racks.

Yield: 6 loaves.

Bourbon Street Beignets

Try filling these delicate French doughnuts with custard or jelly—delightful.

¼ *cup warm water*
(105°F to 115F)
1 *package active dry*
yeast
¼ *cup sugar*
2 *tablespoons*
shortening
½ *teaspoon salt*
½ *cup boiling water*
½ *cup heavy cream*
1 *egg, beaten*
4-4½ *cups all-purpose*
flour
Oil for deep fat
frying
Powdered sugar

Dissolve yeast in warm water; set aside. Place sugar, shortening, salt, and boiling water in bowl. Stir until shortening is melted and sugar dissolves; cool to lukewarm. Add cream, egg, 3 cups flour, and yeast to sugar/shortening mixture. Attach bowl and dough hook. Turn to Speed 2 and mix for 2 minutes. Add remaining flour, ½ cup at a time, until dough clings to hook and cleans sides of bowl, about 5 minutes. Knead on Speed 2 for 5 to 7 minutes longer.

Place dough on lightly floured board and roll into a 10 x 24-inch rectangle. Using a sharp knife, cut dough into 2-inch squares.

In large heavy saucepan or deep fat fryer, heat oil to 360°F. Fry doughnuts, turning to brown on both sides, about 3 minutes. Drain on paper towels and sprinkle with powdered sugar.

Note: Doughnuts can be filled with custard, whipped cream or jelly using a small pastry tube.

Yield: 5 dozen 2-inch doughnuts.

Garlic Pull-Apart Bread

6-7 cups all-purpose flour
3 tablespoons sugar
2 tablespoons garlic salt
2 packages active dry yeast
1½ cups water
½ cup milk
½ cup butter or margarine

Place 5 cups flour, sugar, 1 tablespoon garlic salt, and yeast in bowl. Attach bowl and dough hook. Turn to Speed 2 and mix 30 seconds. Combine water, milk, and ¼ cup butter in a saucepan. Heat over low heat until liquids are very warm (120°F to 130°F).

Turn to Speed 2 and gradually add warm liquids to flour mixture, about 1 minute. Mix 1 minute longer. Continuing on Speed 2, add remaining flour, ½ cup at a time, until dough clings to hook and cleans sides of bowl. Knead on Speed 2 for 5 to 7 minutes longer.

Place in a greased bowl, turning to grease top. Cover; let rise in warm place, free from draft, until doubled in bulk, about 1 hour.

Punch dough down and divide in half. Roll one half to a 12 x 8 x ¼-inch rectangle. Melt remaining butter and mix with remaining garlic salt. Brush dough with mixture. Cut dough into 4 equal strips 8 inches long. Stack strips and cut into 4 equal pieces 2 inches wide. Place pieces on edge in a greased 8½ x 4½ x 2½-inch loaf pan so layers form one row down the length of the pan. Repeat for remaining dough. Cover; let rise in warm place, free from draft, until doubled in bulk, about 1 hour. Bake at 400°F for 30 to 35 minutes. Remove from pans immediately and cool on wire racks.

Yield: 2 loaves.

Carrot Health Bread

4 carrots, peeled and
  cut into 1-inch pieces
⅔ cup milk
3 tablespoons honey
2 teaspoons salt
3 tablespoons butter or
  margarine
1 cup warm water
  (105°F to 115°F)
2 packages active dry
  yeast
3½ cups whole wheat
  flour
3½ cups all-purpose flour
1 egg

Cook carrots in water until very tender. Assemble and attach Fruit/Vegetable Strainer. Turn to Speed 4 and strain carrots. Measure out 1 cup carrot puree and set aside.

Scald milk; stir in honey, salt, and butter. Cool to lukewarm. Dissolve yeast in warm water in warmed bowl. Mix flours together. Add carrot puree, lukewarm milk mixture, and 4½ cups flour mixture to yeast. Attach bowl and dough hook. Turn to Speed 2 and mix 2 minutes, until well blended. Add remaining flour, ½ cup at a time, until dough clings to hook and cleans sides of bowl. Knead on Speed 2 for 7 to 10 minutes longer, or until smooth and elastic.

Place in a greased bowl, turning to grease top. Cover; let rise in warm place, free from draft, until doubled in bulk, about 1 hour.

Punch dough down. Divide dough in half. Shape each half into a loaf. Place each loaf into a greased 8½ x 4½ x 2½-inch loaf pan. Cover; let rise in warm place, free from draft, until doubled in bulk, about 1 hour.

Bake at 400°F for 30 to 35 minutes. Remove from pans immediately and cool on wire racks.

Yield: 2 loaves.

Deli Style Sandwich Rolls

These crusty, hard rolls turn the simplest sandwich filling
into a special luncheon treat.

4½-5½ cups all-purpose
   flour
2 tablespoons sugar
2 teaspoons salt
1 package active dry
   yeast
1½ cups water
3 tablespoons butter or
   margarine
1 egg white, at room
   temperature
   Cornmeal
½ cup water
1 teaspoon cornstarch

Place 4 cups flour, sugar, salt, and yeast in bowl. Attach
bowl and dough hook. Turn to Speed 2 and mix for 1
minute.

Combine 1½ cups water and butter in small saucepan.
Heat over low heat until very warm (120°F to 130°F).

Turn to Speed 2 and gradually add warm liquid to flour
mixture, about 1 minute. Add egg white and mix 2
minutes longer. Continuing on Speed 2, add remaining
flour, ½ cup at a time, until dough clings to hook and
cleans sides of bowl. Knead on Speed 2 for 7 to 10
minutes longer, or until dough is smooth and elastic.

Place in a greased bowl, turning to grease top. Cover; let
rise in warm place, free from draft, until doubled in
bulk, about 45 minutes.

Punch dough down and turn onto floured board. Roll into a 12-inch rope. Cut into twelve 1-inch pieces. Shape
into smooth balls. Place on greased baking sheets,
sprinkled with cornmeal, about 3 inches apart. Cover;
let rise in warm place, free from draft, until doubled in
bulk, about 45 minutes.

Blend ½ cup water into cornstarch in small saucepan
over medium heat. Cook, stirring constantly, until mixture boils. Remove from heat immediately and cool
slightly.

Brush each roll with cornstarch glaze. Slit tops with a
sharp knife crisscross fashion. Bake at 450°F for 15
minutes. Remove from baking sheets immediately and
cool on wire racks.

Yield: 12 rolls.

QUICK BREADS & COOKIES

Here's to the simple life

Corn fritters and pumpkin bread, apple pancakes and gingerbread, shortbread cookies and rich brownies . . . these are the tastes around which special memories are built. In this chapter, find a collection of our favorite down-home treats. Delicious to eat and easy to make, they are sure to be your favorites, too.

Cranberry Bread

1 egg
1 cup orange juice
1 cup sugar
¼ cup shortening,
    melted
3 cups all-purpose flour
4 teaspoons baking
    powder
½ teaspoon salt
1½ teaspoons grated
    orange peel
1 cup chopped fresh
    cranberries
½ cup chopped walnuts

Place egg, orange juice, sugar, and shortening in bowl. Attach bowl and flat beater. Turn to Speed 4 and mix 30 seconds. Stop and scrape bowl.

Combine flour, baking powder, salt, and orange peel. Turn to Speed 2 and add flour mixture to egg mixture, mixing about 15 seconds. Stop and scrape bowl. Fold in cranberries and walnuts.

Spread batter in a greased 9 x 5 x 3-inch loaf pan. Bake at 350°F for 55 to 60 minutes. Remove from pan and cool on wire rack.

Yield: 1 loaf.

Hermits

These old-fashioned cookies laced with molasses, raisins, walnuts and dates improve in flavor if stored several days before eating.

1 cup butter or
    margarine, softened
1½ cups brown sugar
3 eggs
1 tablespoon molasses
1 tablespoon grated
    orange peel
1 teaspoon cloves
1 teaspoon salt
1 teaspoon cinnamon
½ teaspoon ground
    ginger
3 cups all-purpose flour
1 teaspoon baking soda
1 cup chopped walnuts
½ cup chopped raisins
1 cup chopped dates

Place butter, brown sugar, eggs, molasses, orange peel, cloves, salt, cinnamon, and ground ginger in bowl. Attach bowl and flat beater. Turn to Speed 6 and beat 1 minute. Stop and scrape bowl. Return to Speed 6 and beat 30 seconds.

Add flour and baking soda. Turn to Speed 2 and beat 15 seconds. Stop and scrape bowl. Turn to Stir Speed and quickly add walnuts, raisins, and dates, mixing just until blended.

Drop by teaspoonfuls onto greased baking sheets. Bake at 375°F for 12 to 14 minutes. Cool on wire racks.

Yield: 4 dozen cookies.

Banana Nut Bread

⅓ cup shortening
½ cup sugar
2 eggs
1¾ cups sifted all-
    purpose flour
1 teaspoon baking
    powder
½ teaspoon baking soda
½ teaspoon salt
1 cup mashed ripe
    bananas
½ cup chopped walnuts

Place shortening and sugar in bowl. Attach bowl and flat beater. Beat at Speed 6 for 1 minute. Stop and scrape bowl. Beat an additional minute at Speed 6, then turn to Speed 4 and add eggs. Beat 30 seconds. Stop and scrape bowl. Turn to Speed 6 and beat for 1½ minutes.

Sift together flour, baking powder, soda, and salt into a separate bowl. Turn to Stir Speed and add half of flour mixture and half of mashed banana. Mix for 30 seconds, then add remaining flour mixture and banana. Mix an additional 30 seconds. Stop and scrape bowl. Blend walnuts in on Stir Speed, about 15 seconds.

Pour mixture into greased and floured 9 x 5 x 3-inch loaf pan. Bake at 350°F for 40 to 45 minutes. Remove from pan and cool on wire rack.

Yield: 1 loaf.

Mix batter just until the dry ingredients are moistened. Overbeating can result in a tough product with less volume.

Quick breads usually taste and slice better the day after baking. Cool, then wrap and store in a cool place.

For even slices, use a bread knife with a serrated edge. Cut with a gentle sawing motion.

Macaroons

1 can (8 oz.) almond
   paste
2 egg whites
½ cup sugar
1 cup powdered sugar

Place almond paste and egg whites in bowl. Attach bowl and flat beater. Turn to Speed 4 and beat 1 minute. Stop and scrape bowl.

Add sugar. Turn to Speed 4 and beat 30 seconds. Stop and scrape bowl. Sift powdered sugar into bowl. Turn to Speed 6 and beat 15 seconds.

Drop by teaspoonfuls 2 inches apart onto greased and floured baking sheets. Bake at 350°F for 12 to 15 minutes. Cool on wire racks.

Yield: 2 dozen cookies.

Apple Spice Loaf

2 cups all-purpose flour
¾ cup sugar
3 teaspoons baking
   powder
½ teaspoon baking soda
1 teaspoon salt
½ teaspoon cinnamon
¼ teaspoon allspice
⅛ teaspoon cloves
⅛ teaspoon nutmeg
1 egg
2 tablespoons butter or
   margarine, melted
1 cup applesauce

Place flour, sugar, baking powder, soda, salt, cinnamon, allspice, cloves, nutmeg, egg, and butter in bowl. Attach bowl and flat beater. Turn to Speed 4 and beat 15 seconds. Stop and scrape bowl.

Add applesauce. Turn to Speed 4 and beat for 30 seconds. Stop and scrape bowl. Turn to Speed 4 and beat 15 seconds more, until well blended. Spread mixture into a greased 8½ x 4½ x 2½-inch loaf pan. Bake at 350°F for 45 to 55 minutes. Remove from pan and cool on wire rack.

Yield: 1 loaf.

Cream Cheese Brownies

Vanilla and chocolate batter swirled into a rich treat.

1 cup butter or
  margarine, softened
4 squares (1 oz. each)
  unsweetened
  chocolate
2½ cups sugar
4 eggs
1 cup all-purpose flour
½ teaspoon salt
1 cup chopped walnuts
2 teaspoons vanilla
1 package (8 oz.) cream
  cheese, softened

Melt butter and chocolate in double boiler over boiling water. Remove from heat and set aside.

Place 2 cups sugar and 3 eggs in bowl. Attach bowl and flat beater. Turn to Speed 4 and beat a minute and a half. Stop and scrape bowl. Turn to Speed 4 and gradually add chocolate mixture, beating until well blended. Stop and scrape bowl. Add flour, salt, walnuts, and 1 teaspoon vanilla. Turn to Speed 2 and beat 1 minute, until well blended. Remove from bowl and set aside.

Place remaining sugar, egg, vanilla, and cream cheese in clean bowl. Attach bowl and flat beater. Turn to Speed 2 and beat 30 seconds. Stop and scrape bowl. Turn to Speed 6 and beat 1 minute.

Drop chocolate and cream cheese batter by tablespoonfuls into a greased and floured 9 x 13 x 2-inch pan. Swirl lightly with a knife. Bake at 350°F for 45 to 50 minutes. When cool, cut into squares.

Yield: Twenty-four 2 x 2-inch brownies.

Pumpkin Bread

3 cups sugar
1 cup vegetable oil
4 eggs
1 can (16 oz.) pumpkin
3½ cups all-purpose flour
1 teaspoon baking
  powder
2 teaspoons baking
  soda
2 teaspoons salt
1 teaspoon cinnamon
1 teaspoon nutmeg
1 teaspoon allspice
⅔ cup water
½ cup chopped walnuts

Place sugar, oil, and eggs in bowl. Attach bowl and flat beater. Turn to Speed 4 and beat 30 seconds. Stop and scrape bowl. Turn to Speed 4 and beat 10 seconds more.

Add pumpkin, flour, baking powder, soda, salt, cinnamon, nutmeg, and allspice. Turn to Speed 2 and mix 30 seconds. Stop and scrape bowl. Add water and walnuts. Turn to Stir Speed and mix 20 seconds, or until combined.

Pour batter into two greased and floured 9 x 5 x 3-inch loaf pans. Bake at 350°F for 50 to 60 minutes. Remove from pans and cool on wire racks.

Yield: 2 loaves.

Lemon Tea Bread

Lemon peel and walnuts in a moist bread topped with fresh lemon glaze.

½ cup butter or
  margarine, softened
1 cup sugar
2 eggs
2 cups all-purpose flour
1½ teaspoons baking
  powder
¼ teaspoon salt
⅓ cup milk
½ cup chopped walnuts
2 tablespoons grated
  lemon peel

Place butter, sugar, and eggs in bowl. Attach bowl and flat beater. Turn to Speed 6 and beat 1 minute. Stop and scrape bowl.

Combine flour, baking powder, and salt. Turn to Speed 2 and add ⅓ of the flour mixture alternately with ½ the milk, beating 15 seconds after each addition. Repeat until all ingredients are used. Stop and scrape bowl. Turn to Stir Speed and quickly add walnuts and lemon peel.

Pour batter into a greased 8½ x 4½ x 2½-inch loaf pan. Bake at 325°F for 55 to 65 minutes. Brush with *Lemon Glaze* and cool in pan 15 minutes; remove and cool on wire rack.

Yield: 1 loaf.

Lemon Glaze

¼ cup fresh lemon juice
3 tablespoons sugar

Place lemon juice and sugar in small saucepan. Bring to a boil over medium heat and stir until slightly thickened. Remove from heat.

Cinnamon Diamonds

1 cup sugar
¾ cup butter or
  margarine, softened
1 egg
1 teaspoon vanilla
2 cups all-purpose flour
2 teaspoons cinnamon
½ teaspoon baking
  powder
¼ teaspoon salt
1 cup chopped pecans

Place sugar, butter, egg, and vanilla in bowl. Attach bowl and flat beater. Turn to Speed 6 and beat 1 minute. Stop and scrape bowl.

Add flour, cinnamon, baking powder, salt, and pecans. Turn to Speed 2 and mix 30 seconds. Press dough into a greased and floured 8 x 8 x 2-inch pan. Bake at 350°F for 30 to 40 minutes. Cool in pan 10 minutes, then remove and cool on flat surface. When cool, cut into diamonds.

Yield: Sixteen 2 x 2-inch bars.

Zucchini Bread

2 medium zucchini, trimmed

2 cups sugar

1 cup butter or margarine, softened

4 eggs

3 cups all-purpose flour

1 teaspoon cinnamon

¾ teaspoon baking soda

1 teaspoon salt

1 teaspoon baking powder

1 teaspoon grated lemon peel

Assemble and attach Rotor Slicer/Shredder using fine shredder cone (No. 1). Turn to Speed 4 and shred zucchini. Measure out 2 cups and set aside.

Place sugar, butter, and eggs in bowl. Attach bowl and flat beater. Turn to Speed 4 and beat 45 seconds. Stop and scrape bowl. Combine flour, cinnamon, soda, salt, and baking powder. Add flour mixture to bowl. Turn to Speed 2 and mix 15 seconds. Stop and scrape bowl. Add zucchini and lemon peel and mix on Speed 2 for 15 seconds.

Spread batter into two greased and floured 8½ x 4½ x 2½-inch loaf pans. Bake at 350°F for 50 to 60 minutes. Remove from pans and cool on wire rack.

Yield: 2 loaves.

Pecan Bread

Nutty and rich with buttermilk.

1 egg

1 teaspoon orange juice

¾ cup sugar

3 tablespoons butter or margarine, melted

3 cups all-purpose flour

2½ teaspoons baking powder

½ teaspoon baking soda

½ teaspoon salt

1½ teaspoons grated orange peel

1½ cups buttermilk

1½ cups chopped pecans

Place egg, orange juice, sugar, and butter in bowl. Attach bowl and wire whip. Turn to Speed 4 and whip 30 seconds. Stop and scrape bowl.

Combine flour, baking powder, soda, salt, and orange peel. Turn to Speed 2 and add flour mixture, mixing about 15 seconds. Stop and scrape bowl. Add buttermilk. Turn to Speed 4 and whip 20 seconds. Reduce to Stir Speed and quickly add pecans, mixing just until combined.

Spread batter in a greased and floured 9 x 5 x 3-inch loaf pan. Bake at 350°F for 55 to 65 minutes. Remove from pan and cool on wire rack.

Yield: 1 loaf.

Orange Muffins

⅓ cup butter or
  margarine
½ cup sugar
 1 egg
 1 teaspoon grated
  orange peel
½ cup orange juice
¼ cup milk
 2 cups all-purpose flour
 2 teaspoons baking
  powder
½ teaspoon baking soda
½ teaspoon salt

Place butter and sugar in bowl. Attach bowl and flat beater. Turn to Speed 6 and beat 1 minute. Stop and scrape bowl. Add egg, orange peel, orange juice, and milk. Turn to Speed 4 and beat 30 seconds.

Combine flour, baking powder, soda, and salt, and add to bowl. Turn to Speed 2 and mix 15 seconds, or just until moistened. *Do not overbeat.*

Fill greased muffin tins two-thirds full. Bake at 400°F for 20 to 25 minutes. Serve warm.

Yield: 12 muffins.

Apricot Nut Pancakes

½ cup dried apricots
¾ cup milk
 2 tablespoons butter or
  margarine, melted
 1 egg
⅔ cup whole wheat
  flour
⅓ cup all-purpose flour
 2 teaspoons baking
  powder
 2 tablespoons sugar
¼ teaspoon salt
½ cup finely chopped
  walnuts

Assemble and attach Food Grinder using fine grinding plate. Turn to Speed 4 and grind apricots; set aside.

Place milk, butter, and egg in bowl. Attach bowl and wire whip. Turn to Speed 6 and whip 30 seconds. Combine whole wheat flour, all-purpose flour, baking powder, sugar, and salt. Add to milk mixture. Turn to Speed 2 and whip 20 seconds. Stop and scrape bowl. Turn to Speed 6 and whip 15 seconds or until well blended. Reduce to Stir Speed and quickly fold in apricots and walnuts.

Slowly heat greased griddle or heavy skillet. Using 2 tablespoons batter for each pancake, drop onto griddle. Cook until bubbles form on surface and edges become dry. Turn and cook until golden brown on underside. Serve immediately.

Yield: 12 pancakes.

Blondies

Quite simply . . . a blonde brownie.

½ cup plus 2 tablespoons
  butter or margarine
2 cups brown sugar
2 eggs
1½ teaspoons vanilla
2 cups all-purpose flour
1½ teaspoons baking
  powder
½ teaspoon salt
½ cup chopped walnuts
¼ cup semi-sweet
  chocolate chips

Place butter, brown sugar, eggs, and vanilla in bowl. Attach bowl and flat beater. Turn to Speed 4 and beat 1 minute. Stop and scrape bowl.

Add flour, baking powder, and salt. Turn to Speed 2 and beat 15 seconds. Stop and scrape bowl. Turn to Stir Speed and quickly add nuts and chocolate chips, mixing just until combined.

Press dough into a 9 x 13 x 2-inch greased and floured pan. Bake at 350°F for 25 to 35 minutes. Cool in pan, then cut into bars.

Yield: Twenty-four 2 x 2-inch bars.

Boston Brown Bread

New Englanders have served up this bread with their Saturday-night baked beans for generations. Delicious served warm with butter or cream cheese.

---

1 cup rye berries or 1
  cup rye flour
1 cup corn kernels or 1
  cup cornmeal
1 cup graham flour
¾ tablespoon baking
  soda
2 teaspoons salt
¾ cup molasses
2 cups buttermilk

Assemble and attach Grain Mill. Set Mill on Click 3. Turn to Speed 10 and grind rye berries and corn kernels. Set aside.

Place rye flour, cornmeal, graham flour, baking soda, and salt in bowl. Attach bowl and flat beater. Turn to Stir Speed and mix 30 seconds. Add molasses and buttermilk. Turn to Speed 2 and mix 1 minute or until well combined.

Pour batter ⅔ full into 2 well-greased 1 pound coffee cans. Cover cans with foil and tie to make watertight. Place cans on rack in large kettle. Add water until bottom half of cans are submerged.

Cover kettle tightly and steam 1½ to 2 hours, or until pick inserted in center comes out clean. Add more water if needed. Remove bread from cans and serve warm.

Yield: 2 loaves.

Scones

A rich biscuit; perfect for fresh fruit shortcake.

2 cups all-purpose flour
2 tablespoons sugar
2 teaspoons baking
  powder
½ teaspoon salt
⅓ cup butter or
  margarine, softened
2 eggs
½ cup heavy cream
1 teaspoon water

Place flour, sugar, baking powder, salt, and butter in bowl. Attach bowl and flat beater. Turn to Speed 2 and beat 30 seconds or until well blended. Stop and scrape bowl.

Add 1 egg and cream. Turn to Speed 2 and beat 30 seconds or until soft dough forms. Knead dough 3 times on a lightly floured surface. Divide dough in half. Pat each half into a circle, about ½-inch thick. Cut each circle into 8 wedges.

Place wedges 2 inches apart on greased baking sheets. Beat remaining egg and water together. Brush egg mixture over each wedge. Bake at 425°F for 10 to 12 minutes. Serve immediately.

Yield: 16 scones.

Popovers

Crusty on the outside, but oh so moist and tender on the inside!

2 eggs
1 cup milk
1 tablespoon butter or
  margarine, melted
1 cup all-purpose flour
¼ teaspoon salt

Place eggs, milk, butter, flour, and salt in bowl. Attach bowl and wire whip. Turn to Speed 4 and beat 15 seconds. Stop and scrape bowl. Turn to Speed 4 and beat 15 seconds more.

Fill 8 heavily greased and floured custard cups ½ full with batter. Place cups on a cookie sheet. Place cookie sheet in a cold oven and set heat at 450°F. Bake for 15 minutes; reduce heat to 350°F and bake 20 to 25 minutes longer. Remove from oven and cut slit into side of each popover. Serve immediately.

Yield: 8 popovers.

Raisin-Wheat Muffins

1¾ cups wheat berries or
  2 cups whole wheat
  flour
2 eggs
⅓ cup yogurt
⅔ cup warm milk
⅓ cup honey
⅓ cup vegetable oil
¾ teaspoon salt
1 teaspoon baking soda
½ cup raisins

Assemble and attach Grain Mill. Set Mill on Click 3. Turn to Speed 10 and grind berries. Set aside.

Place eggs in bowl. Attach bowl and wire whip. Turn to Speed 2 and beat 15 seconds. Add yogurt and milk. Turn to Speed 4 and beat 15 seconds.

Add honey, oil, flour, salt, baking soda, and raisins. Turn to Speed 2 and mix until well blended, about 15 seconds.

Pour batter into ungreased muffin tins. Bake at 425°F for 15 minutes.

Yield: 18 muffins.

Cajun Gingerbread

Delectable topped with Eggnog Sauce, fresh whipped cream or homemade apple butter.

½ cup sugar
½ cup butter or
  margarine, softened
1 egg
½ cup molasses
1½ cups all-purpose flour
¾ teaspoon baking soda
½ teaspoon cinnamon
1 teaspoon ground
  ginger
¾ teaspoon salt
¼ teaspoon cloves
½ cup boiling water

Place sugar and butter in bowl. Attach bowl and flat beater. Turn to Speed 6 and beat 15 seconds. Stop and scrape bowl. Add egg and molasses. Turn to Speed 4 and beat 30 seconds, until well combined.

Combine flour, soda, cinnamon, ground ginger, salt, and cloves. Turn to Speed 2 and add ⅓ of the flour mixture alternately with ½ of the water, beating 10 seconds after each addition. Repeat until all ingredients are used. Stop and scrape bowl. Turn to Speed 4 and beat 10 seconds.

Pour batter into a greased 8 x 8 x 2-inch pan. Bake at 350°F for 35 to 40 minutes. Serve warm.

Yield: 9 servings.

German Apple Pancakes

Diced apple, cloves and cinnamon make these pancakes
a special breakfast treat.

1 cup all-purpose flour
1 cup apple, peeled and
 diced
¾ cup milk
1 egg
2 tablespoons sugar
2 teaspoons baking
 powder
¼ teaspoon salt
⅛ teaspoon cinnamon
 Dash cloves

Place all ingredients in bowl. Attach bowl and wire
whip. Turn to Speed 6 and whip 30 seconds. Stop and
scrape bowl. Turn to Speed 6 and whip 15 seconds, or
until smooth.

Slowly heat greased griddle or heavy skillet. Using
2 tablespoons batter for each pancake, drop onto griddle.
Cook until bubbles form on surface and edges become
dry. Turn and cook until golden brown on underside.
Serve immediately.

Yield: 12 to 16 pancakes.

Pecan Shortbread Cookies

1 cup butter or
 margarine, softened
1 teaspoon vanilla
¾ cup brown sugar
2½ cups all-purpose flour
½ cup chopped pecans

Place butter, vanilla, and brown sugar in bowl. Attach
bowl and flat beater. Turn to Speed 6 and beat 1 minute.
Stop and scrape bowl.

Turn to Speed 2 and add flour, beat 30 seconds. Stop and
scrape bowl. Turn to Stir Speed and quickly add pecans,
mixing just until blended.

Shape dough into a log 1½-inches in diameter. Wrap in
waxed paper and chill 20 minutes. Slice dough ½-inch
thick. Place on greased baking sheets. Bake at 325°F for
18 to 20 minutes. Cool on wire racks.

Yield: 2 dozen cookies.

Soft cookies should be stored between layers of waxed paper in an airtight
container. A piece of apple or bread, changed frequently, will help keep
cookies soft. Store crisp cookies in a container with a loose-fitting lid. If
they soften, place them in an oven at 300°F for 3-5 minutes before
serving.

Orange Tea Biscuits

Surprise your guests with these light, fluffy biscuits
"iced" with a sweet orange glaze.

2 cups flour
2½ teaspoons baking
   powder
½ teaspoon salt
3 teaspoons grated
   orange peel
3 tablespoons sugar
½ cup shortening
⅔ cup milk

Place all ingredients except milk in bowl. Attach bowl
and flat beater. Turn to Stir Speed and cut shortening in,
about 1 minute. Stop and scrape bowl.

Add milk and mix on Stir Speed until dough starts to cling
to beater. Avoid overbeating. Turn dough onto lightly
floured board and knead until smooth, about 30 seconds.
Pat or roll to ½-inch thickness. Cut with floured 2-inch
biscuit cutter.

Place 2 inches apart on greased baking sheets. Bake at
425°F for 12 to 15 minutes. Brush with *Orange Glaze*
while hot. Serve immediately.

Yield: 12 biscuits.

Orange Glaze

1 tablespoon butter
2 tablespoons orange
   juice
1 tablespoon sugar

Melt butter in small saucepan over medium heat. Add
orange juice and sugar. Cook, stirring constantly, until
mixture boils. Remove from heat immediately and cool.

Whole Wheat Pancakes

¾ cup milk
2 tablespoons butter or
   margarine, melted
1 egg
⅓ cup whole wheat
   flour
⅔ cup all-purpose flour
2 teaspoons baking
   powder
2 tablespoons sugar
¼ teaspoon salt

Place milk, butter, and egg in bowl. Attach bowl and
wire whip. Turn to Speed 4 and whip 30 seconds. Add
whole wheat flour, all-purpose flour, baking powder,
sugar, and salt. Turn to Speed 6 and whip 30 seconds, until
combined.

Slowly heat greased griddle or heavy skillet. Using
2 tablespoons batter for each pancake, drop onto griddle.
Cook until bubbles form on surface and edges become
dry. Turn and cook until golden brown on underside.
Serve immediately.

Yield: 10 pancakes.

Carrot Oatmeal Cookies

A new twist on a time-honored recipe.

¾ cup butter or
    margarine, melted
¾ cup brown sugar
¾ cup sugar
1 egg
1 cup shredded carrots
¼ cup water
2 cups rolled oats
2 cups all-purpose flour
1 teaspoon baking soda
½ teaspoon salt

Place butter, brown sugar, sugar, and egg in bowl. Attach bowl and flat beater. Turn to Speed 6 and beat 1 minute. Stop and scrape bowl.

Add carrots and water. Turn to Speed 4 and beat 15 seconds. Stop and scrape bowl. Add oats, flour, soda, and salt. Turn to Speed 4 and beat 15 seconds.

Drop by teaspoonfuls on greased baking sheets, 2 inches apart. Bake at 375°F for 8 to 10 minutes. Cool on wire racks.

Yield: 4 dozen cookies.

Sour Cream Soda Bread

Raisins, caraway seeds and sour cream give this traditional Irish loaf its special flavor.

2 cups all-purpose flour
¾ teaspoon baking soda
½ teaspoon salt
3 tablespoons sugar
½ cup butter or
    margarine, softened
½ cup raisins
1 tablespoon caraway
    seeds
1 cup sour cream
1 tablespoon milk

Place flour, soda, salt, sugar, and butter in bowl. Attach bowl and flat beater. Turn to Speed 4 and mix 2 minutes or until mixture is crumbly. Stop and scrape bowl.

Add raisins, caraway seeds, and sour cream. Turn to Speed 2 and beat 1 minute or until well blended. Form dough into a mound-shaped circle on a greased baking sheet. Brush dough with milk. Bake at 375°F for 45 to 55 minutes. Remove from baking sheet and cool on wire rack.

Yield: 1 loaf.

Spoon Bread

A heavy cornmeal soufflé; excellent with chicken or fried fish.

1 cup cornmeal
½ teaspoon salt
½ cup water
1½ cups milk
2 eggs
3 tablespoons butter or margarine, melted

Combine cornmeal, salt, water, and milk in a large saucepan. Cook and stir over medium heat until mixture thickens; set aside.

Place eggs in bowl. Attach bowl and wire whip. Turn to Speed 8 and whip 15 seconds. Reduce to Speed 4 and add cornmeal mixture, a tablespoon at a time, until completely incorporated, about 3 minutes. Stop and scrape bowl. Turn to Speed 4 and whip an additional 15 seconds.

Pour batter into a greased 1-quart casserole. Bake at 375°F for 50 to 60 minutes. Serve immediately.

Yield: 6 to 8 servings.

Brown Edge Wafers

Crisp, buttery cookies with just a hint of orange.

½ cup butter or margarine, softened
½ cup sugar
1 egg
1 teaspoon vanilla
½ teaspoon grated orange peel
1 cup all-purpose flour

Place butter and sugar in bowl. Attach bowl and flat beater. Turn to Speed 6 and beat 15 seconds. Stop and scrape bowl.

Add egg, vanilla, and orange peel. Turn to Speed 6 and beat 30 seconds, until fluffy. Stop and scrape bowl. Turn to Speed 2 and add flour, mixing 15 seconds or just until blended.

Drop by teaspoonfuls onto greased baking sheets. Bake at 375°F for 8 to 10 minutes. Cool on wire racks.

Yield: 2 dozen wafers.

Corn Fritters

1½ cups all-purpose flour
2 tablespoons sugar
2 teaspoons baking powder
½ teaspoon salt
¼ cup milk
2 eggs
1 can (8 oz.) cream-style corn
1 tablespoon butter or margarine, melted
Vegetable oil for deep fat frying

Place all ingredients except vegetable oil in bowl. Attach bowl and flat beater. Turn to Speed 2 and beat 30 seconds. Stop and scrape bowl. Turn to Speed 6 and beat 15 seconds.

Heat oil in a 1½-quart saucepan over medium-high heat to 375°F. Drop batter in oil, a tablespoon at a time. Turn fritters once after bubbles form on top and continue frying until golden brown. Serve immediately with maple syrup.

Yield: 24 fritters.

Meringue Cookies

Sweet peaks of meringue with the tangy taste of apricots.

2 egg whites
2 cups powdered sugar
1 teaspoon cider vinegar
1 teaspoon vanilla
1 cup finely chopped walnuts
1 cup finely chopped dried apricots

Place egg whites in bowl. Attach bowl and wire whip. Turn to Speed 8 and whip until soft peaks form. Reduce to Speed 4 and gradually add powdered sugar, about 1 minute; whip until well blended. Stop and scrape bowl.

Turn to Speed 10 and add vinegar and vanilla; whip 1 minute. Reduce to Stir Speed and quickly add nuts and apricots, mixing just until blended.

Drop by tablespoonfuls onto greased and floured baking sheets. Bake at 300°F for 15 to 17 minutes. Cool on wire racks.

Yield: 2½ dozen cookies.

CAKES & FROSTINGS

They make an occasion special

For birthdays, anniversaries, housewarmings, or holiday celebrations, there is no substitute for a home-baked cake. Whether it's a cheese-cake, chocolate cake, a moist fruitcake, or a lavishly decorated torte, it's always extra-special when it's made with a dash of tender loving care . . . and your KitchenAid mixer.

Buttermilk Spice Cake

3 cups all-purpose flour
2 cups sugar
3 teaspoons baking powder
¾ teaspoon baking soda
¾ teaspoon salt
2 teaspoons cinnamon
½ teaspoon mace
¾ cup butter or margarine, softened
2 teaspoons vanilla
1 cup buttermilk
4 eggs
1 cup chopped pecans

Sift flour, sugar, baking powder, soda, salt, cinnamon, and mace into bowl. Make a well in dry ingredients and add butter, vanilla, and ⅔ cup of buttermilk.

Attach bowl and flat beater. Turn to Stir Speed and mix 1 minute. Stop and scrape bowl. Turn to Speed 4 and beat 2 minutes.

Add remaining buttermilk and eggs. Turn to Speed 2 and mix 30 seconds. Stop and scrape bowl. Turn to Speed 4 and beat 1 minute. Reduce to Stir Speed and quickly add pecans, about 15 seconds.

Pour batter into a greased and floured 10-inch bundt pan. Bake at 375°for 40 to 45 minutes. Cool in pan 10 minutes, then remove and cool on wire racks.

Yield: One 10-inch cake.

Sour Cream Bundt Cake

3 cups all-purpose flour
½ teaspoon salt
3 teaspoons baking powder
1 teaspoon baking soda
1½ cups sugar
1 teaspoon cinnamon
1 cup butter or margarine, softened
1 cup sour cream
1 teaspoon vanilla
3 eggs
1 cup chopped nuts

Sift flour, salt, baking powder, soda, sugar, and cinnamon into bowl. Add butter, sour cream, and vanilla. Attach bowl and flat beater. Turn to Stir Speed and mix until ingredients are combined, about 30 seconds. Stop and scrape bowl. Turn to Speed 4 and beat for 1½ minutes. Stop and scrape bowl.

Turn to Stir Speed and add eggs, one at a time, beating 15 seconds after each addition. Turn to Speed 2 and beat 30 seconds. Reduce to Stir Speed and quickly add nuts, about 15 seconds.

Pour batter into greased and floured 10-inch bundt pan. Bake at 350°F for 60 to 65 minutes. Cool in pan 10 minutes, then remove and cool on wire racks.

Yield: One 10-inch cake.

Marble Cheesecake

You won't be able to resist this beautiful temptation.

1 cup graham cracker crumbs

¼ cup brown sugar

3 tablespoons butter or margarine, melted

4 packages (8 oz. each) cream cheese, softened

2 teaspoons vanilla

1¾ cups sugar

4 eggs

2 squares (1 oz. each) unsweetened chocolate, melted

Place graham cracker crumbs, brown sugar, and butter in bowl. Attach bowl and flat beater. Turn to Speed 2 and mix 30 seconds. Press mixture into the bottom of 9-inch springform pan.

Place cream cheese, vanilla, and sugar in clean bowl. Attach bowl and flat beater. Turn to Speed 6 and beat 2 minutes, until fluffy. Stop and scrape bowl. Turn to Speed 2 and add eggs, one at a time, beating 15 seconds after each addition. Stop and scrape bowl. Turn to Speed 4 and beat 15 seconds.

Pour ⅓ of cream cheese mixture into a small bowl. Add chocolate and mix well. Drop chocolate and plain batter by the spoonful into prepared pan. Swirl lightly with a knife. Bake at 325°F for 1 hour 30 minutes. Cool on wire rack 30 minutes, then refrigerate at least 2 hours.

Yield: One 9-inch cake.

Old-Fashioned Pound Cake

This simple yet versatile cake has just the slightest hint of lemon.
Serve it plain, with fresh fruit or a sprinkling of powdered sugar.

2¼ cups all-purpose flour

1 teaspoon baking powder

1 teaspoon salt

1¼ cups sugar

1 tablespoon grated lemon peel

⅔ cup butter or margarine, softened

½ cup milk

1 tablespoon lemon juice

3 eggs

Place flour, baking powder, salt, sugar, and lemon peel in bowl. Make a well in the center and add butter and milk. Attach bowl and flat beater. Turn to Stir Speed and mix 30 seconds to combine. Stop and scrape bowl. Turn to Speed 4 and beat 1 minute.

Add lemon juice and eggs. Turn to Speed 2 and beat 30 seconds. Stop and scrape bowl. Turn to Speed 6 and beat 1 minute, until fluffy.

Pour batter into a greased and floured 9 x 5 x 3-inch loaf pan. Bake at 325°F for 1 hour 10 minutes. Cool in pan 10 minutes, then remove and cool on wire rack.

Yield: One 9-inch loaf.

Chocolate Roll

4 eggs, separated
¾ cup sugar
½ teaspoon vanilla
⅔ cup cake flour
1 teaspoon baking
  powder
¼ teaspoon salt
¼ cup cocoa

Place egg yolks in bowl. Attach bowl and wire whip. Turn to Speed 8 and whip 2 minutes, until light and lemon colored. Continuing on Speed 8, gradually sprinkle in ¼ cup sugar and vanilla and beat 2 minutes more. Remove from bowl and set aside.

Place egg whites in clean bowl. Attach bowl and wire whip. Turn to Speed 8 and whip until whites begin to hold shape. Continuing on Speed 8, gradually sprinkle in remaining sugar, whipping until stiff but not dry.

Fold egg yolk mixture into egg whites. Sift flour, baking powder, salt, and cocoa together. Fold into egg mixture.

Line a 10½ x 15½ x 1-inch jelly roll pan with waxed paper and grease. Pour batter into pan and bake at 375°F for 10 to 12 minutes. Remove from oven and immediately turn onto a towel sprinkled with powdered sugar. Remove waxed paper, and roll cake and towel together; cool completely.

When cool, unroll cake and spread with *Whipped Cream Filling*. Reroll and sprinkle with powdered sugar.

Yield: Ten 1-inch servings.

Whipped Cream Filling

1 cup heavy cream
½ teaspoon vanilla
3 tablespoons sugar

Place cream and vanilla in bowl. Attach bowl and wire whip. Turn to Speed 8 and whip until cream begins to thicken. Continuing on Speed 8, gradually sprinkle in sugar, whipping until stiff.

Do not substitute shortening or vegetable oil in recipes which specifically call for butter or margarine.

For best results, all ingredients should be at room temperature.

Use only large eggs in each recipe.

Light-N-Luscious Lemon Pavé

Layers of feather-light sponge cake filled with a tangy Lemon Filling
and decorated with Lemon Buttercream Frosting.

4 eggs, separated
¾ cup sugar
*½ tablespoon vegetable
  oil*
1 teaspoon vanilla
¾ cup cake flour
*1 teaspoon baking
  powder*
½ teaspoon salt

Place egg whites in bowl. Attach bowl and wire whip.
Turn to Speed 8 and whip until stiff but not dry. Remove
from bowl and set aside.

Place egg yolks and sugar in bowl. Attach bowl and wire
whip. Turn to Speed 6 and whip 1 minute or until thick
and lemon colored. Stop and scrape bowl. Add oil and
vanilla. Turn to Speed 4 and whip 30 seconds. Gently
fold egg whites into egg yolk mixture.

Sift flour, baking powder, and salt together. Fold half of
flour mixture into egg mixture. Repeat with remaining
flour.

Pour batter into a 10 x 15 x 1-inch jelly roll pan which
has been lined with waxed paper, greased and floured.
Bake at 375°F for 10 to 12 minutes. Immediately loosen
cake from pan and invert onto a towel sprinkled with
cake flour; cool completely.

Cut cake crosswise to form three 5 x 10 x 1-inch layers.
Spread *Lemon Filling* between layers. Cover cake tightly
with plastic wrap and refrigerate at least 4 hours. Frost
and decorate with *Lemon Buttercream Frosting*, page 148.

Yield: Ten 1-inch servings.

Lemon Filling

5 egg yolks
⅓ cup sugar
⅓ cup lemon juice
*4 tablespoons butter or
  margarine*
*1 teaspoon grated fresh
  lemon peel*
½ cup heavy cream

Combine egg yolks, sugar, and lemon juice in double
boiler over boiling water. Cook, stirring constantly until
mixture is very thick, about 5 minutes; *do not boil.*
Remove from heat.

Add butter, 1 tablespoon at a time, beating until
thoroughly incorporated. Stir in lemon peel. Cover
mixture and refrigerate 1 hour.

Place cream in bowl. Attach bowl and wire whip. Turn
to Speed 10 and whip until stiff. Fold whipped cream into
egg mixture. Refrigerate until ready to use.

Hazelnut Torte

Light-as-air layers made with finely ground hazelnuts
and bread crumbs and spread with a Creamy Mocha Filling.

6 eggs, separated
¾ cup sugar
⅓ cup plain bread
   crumbs
¼ cup all-purpose flour
⅔ cup finely chopped
   hazelnuts

Place egg whites in bowl. Attach bowl and wire whip. Turn to Speed 8 and whip until soft peaks form. Continuing on Speed 8, gradually sprinkle in ¼ cup sugar, whipping until stiff peaks form. Remove from bowl and set aside.

Place egg yolks in clean bowl. Attach bowl and flat beater. Turn to Speed 8 and beat 2 minutes, until thick and lemon colored. Reduce to Speed 6 and gradually sprinkle in remaining sugar; beat 1 minute. Stop and scrape bowl.

Add bread crumbs, flour, and nuts. Turn to Speed 2 and beat 30 seconds, until well blended. Fold egg white mixture into egg yolk mixture.

Pour batter into a greased and floured 9-inch springform pan. Bake at 325°F for 40 to 45 minutes. Cool in pan 10 minutes, then remove and cool completely on wire rack.

When cool, slice cake in thirds to form 3 layers. Frost with *Creamy Mocha Filling.*

Yield: One 9-inch torte.

Creamy Mocha Filling

2 squares (1 oz. each)
   semi-sweet chocolate,
   melted
1 cup butter or
   margarine, softened
2 cups powdered sugar
2 teaspoons instant
   coffee
1 teaspoon vanilla

Place chocolate and butter in bowl. Attach bowl and flat beater. Turn to Speed 4 and beat 2 minutes. Sift sugar and coffee into bowl. Add vanilla. Turn to Speed 2 and mix 15 seconds. Stop and scrape bowl. Turn to Speed 6 and beat 2 minutes, until light and fluffy.

Yield: 2 cups.

German Chocolate Cake

½ cup hot water
4 squares (1 oz. each) semi-sweet chocolate
1 cup butter or margarine, softened
2 cups sugar
4 eggs
2¼ cups all-purpose flour
1 teaspoon baking soda
½ teaspoon salt
1 cup buttermilk
1 teaspoon vanilla

Place water and chocolate in double boiler. Stir constantly over boiling water until chocolate melts; set aside.

Place butter and sugar in bowl. Attach bowl and flat beater. Turn to Speed 6 and beat 2 minutes, until fluffy. Stop and scrape bowl. Turn to Speed 4 and add eggs, one at a time, beating 15 seconds after each addition. Continuing on Speed 4, add chocolate mixture, and beat 15 seconds more. Stop and scrape bowl.

Add flour, soda, salt, buttermilk, and vanilla. Turn to Speed 2 and mix until well blended, about 30 seconds.

Pour batter into two greased and floured 9-inch cake pans. Bake at 350°F for 35 to 45 minutes. Cool in pans 10 minutes, then remove and cool on wire racks. Frost middle layer and top with *Coconut Pecan Frosting*.

Yield: One 9-inch cake.

Coconut Pecan Frosting

1 cup sugar
¾ cup evaporated milk
3 eggs, beaten
⅓ cup butter or margarine
1 cup shredded coconut
1 cup chopped pecans

Combine sugar, evaporated milk, eggs, and butter in a large saucepan. Cook and stir over medium heat until mixture begins to thicken.

Remove from heat and place in bowl. Add coconut and pecans. Attach bowl and flat beater. Turn to Speed 2 and beat until thick and spreadable. Refrigerate until ready to use.

Yield: 3 cups.

Carrot Cake

4 eggs
1 cup butter or
  margarine, melted
2 cups all-purpose flour
1½ cups sugar
1½ teaspoons baking
  powder
¼ teaspoon salt
1 teaspoon cinnamon
2½ cups finely grated
  carrots
½ cup chopped walnuts

Place eggs and butter in bowl. Attach bowl and flat beater. Turn to Speed 6 and beat 1 minute. Stop and scrape bowl. Add flour, sugar, baking powder, salt, and cinnamon. Turn to Speed 2 and beat 30 seconds, until combined. Reduce to Stir Speed and quickly fold in carrots and walnuts, about 10 seconds.

Pour batter into a greased and floured 9-inch springform pan. Bake at 350°F for 1 hour 15 minutes. Cake is very moist and should not be tested for doneness with an inserted toothpick. Remove cake from oven at end of baking period.

Cool in pan 10 minutes, then remove and cool on wire rack. When cool, slice cake in half to form two layers. Frost with *Cream Cheese Frosting*.

Yield: One 9-inch cake.

Cream Cheese Frosting

4 packages (3 oz. each)
  cream cheese,
  softened
¼ cup butter or
  margarine, softened
2 teaspoons vanilla
2½ cups powdered sugar

Place cream cheese, butter, and vanilla in bowl. Attach bowl and flat beater. Turn to Speed 6 and beat 2 minutes. Stop and scrape bowl.

Sift powdered sugar into bowl. Turn to Speed 2 and beat 30 seconds, just until combined. Stop and scrape bowl. Turn to Speed 6 and beat 2 minutes. Refrigerate until ready to use.

Yield: 3 cups.

Wacky Chocolate Bundt Cake

Don't be thrown by the name or unusual list of ingredients.
This is a chocolate lover's delight.

2¼ cups all-purpose flour
1½ cups sugar
4½ tablespoons cocoa
1½ teaspoons baking
   soda
¾ teaspoon salt
½ cup vegetable oil
1½ tablespoons white
   vinegar
1½ teaspoons vanilla
1¼ cups milk
2 tablespoons dark rum

Sift flour, sugar, cocoa, soda, and salt into bowl. Make a well and add oil, vinegar, and vanilla. Attach bowl and flat beater. Turn to Speed 2 and beat 30 seconds. Stop and scrape bowl.

Add milk and rum. Turn to Speed 2 and beat 30 seconds. Stop and scrape bowl. Turn to Speed 6 and beat 1 minute.

Pour batter into a greased and floured 10-inch bundt pan. Bake at 350°F for 50 to 55 minutes. Cool in pan 10 minutes, then remove and cool on wire racks.

Yield: One 10-inch cake.

Banana Nut Spice Cake

2⅓ cups all-purpose flour
1⅔ cups sugar
1¼ teaspoons baking
   powder
1¼ teaspoons baking
   soda
1 teaspoon salt
½ teaspoon cinnamon
¼ teaspoon cloves
¼ teaspoon nutmeg
⅔ cup shortening
1¼ cups mashed ripe
   banana
⅔ cup buttermilk
1 teaspoon vanilla
2 eggs
⅓ cup chopped walnuts

Sift flour, sugar, baking powder, soda, salt, cinnamon, cloves, and nutmeg into bowl. Make a well and add shortening, banana, and ⅓ cup buttermilk. Turn to Stir Speed and mix 30 seconds. Stop and scrape bowl. Turn to Speed 4 and beat 1 minute.

Add remaining buttermilk, vanilla, and eggs. Turn to Speed 2 and beat 30 seconds. Stop and scrape bowl. Turn to Speed 4 and beat 1 minute. Reduce to Stir Speed and quickly add nuts, mixing just until blended.

Pour batter into two greased and floured 9-inch cake pans. Bake at 350°F for 35 to 40 minutes. Cool in pans 10 minutes, then remove and cool on wire racks. Frost with *Buttercream Frosting*, page 148.

Yield: One 9-inch cake.

Golden Fruit Cake

1½ cups butter or
   margarine, softened
2½ cups brown sugar
   5 eggs
3½ cups all-purpose flour
1¼ teaspoons baking
   powder
   1 teaspoon salt
   2 teaspoons cinnamon
   ¼ teaspoon cloves
   1 jar (10 oz.) currant
   jelly
   ½ cup orange juice
   1 tablespoon grated
   orange peel
1¼ cups seedless raisins
   1 cup candied red
   cherries, chopped
1½ cups chopped
   walnuts
   1 package (6 oz.) dried
   apricots, chopped
   ½ cup pitted dates,
   chopped

Place butter, brown sugar, and eggs in bowl. Attach bowl and flat beater. Turn to Speed 4 and beat 2 minutes. Stop and scrape bowl.

Sift flour, baking powder, salt, cinnamon, and cloves together; set aside. Combine jelly, orange juice, and orange peel together in a small bowl. Turn to Speed 2 and add flour mixture in 3 parts, alternating with the jelly mixture; mix 15 seconds after each addition. Repeat until all ingredients are used. Reduce to Stir Speed and quickly add raisins, cherries, walnuts, apricots, and dates, mixing just until blended.

Pour batter into three 8½ x 4½ x 2½-inch loaf pans which have been lined with several thicknesses of waxed paper. Bake at 300°F for 2 hours. Cool in pans. When cool, wrap cakes well and store 2 to 3 weeks to mellow flavor.

Yield: 3 loaves.

Buttercream Frosting

¾ cup butter or
    margarine, softened
2 cups powdered sugar
1½ teaspoons vanilla

Place butter in bowl. Attach bowl and flat beater. Turn to Speed 6 and beat 30 seconds. Stop and scrape bowl.

Sift powdered sugar into bowl. Add vanilla. Turn to Speed 2 and beat 30 seconds. Stop and scrape bowl. Turn to Speed 6 and beat 2 minutes, until fluffy.

Yield: 2 cups.

Buttercream Frosting Variations

Lemon Buttercream Frosting

1¼ cups butter or
    margarine, softened
2 teaspoons grated
    lemon peel
3 tablespoons lemon
    juice
3 cups powdered sugar

Place butter, lemon peel, and lemon juice in bowl. Attach bowl and flat beater. Turn to Speed 6 and beat 30 seconds. Stop and scrape bowl.

Sift powdered sugar into bowl. Turn to Speed 2 and beat 30 seconds. Stop and scrape bowl. Turn to Speed 6 and beat 2 minutes, until fluffy.

Yield: 3 cups.

Maple Walnut Buttercream Frosting

1 cup butter or
    margarine, softened
2¾ cups powdered sugar
2 tablespoons brown
    sugar
2 tablespoons maple
    syrup
¼ cup chopped walnuts

Place butter in bowl. Attach bowl and flat beater. Turn to Speed 6 and beat 30 seconds. Stop and scrape bowl.

Sift powdered sugar into bowl. Turn to Speed 2 and beat 30 seconds. Stop and scrape bowl. Add brown sugar and syrup. Turn to Speed 6 and beat 2 minutes, until fluffy. Reduce to Stir Speed and quickly add nuts.

Yield: 3 cups.

Brenda's Pumpkin Cake Roll

Spicy pumpkin cake rolled with a sweetened cream cheese filling.

3 eggs
1 cup sugar
⅔ cup pumpkin
¾ cup all-purpose flour
1 teaspoon baking
powder
2 teaspoons cinnamon
½ teaspoon nutmeg
1 teaspoon ground
ginger

Place eggs in bowl. Attach bowl and flat beater. Turn to Speed 6 and beat 1 minute. Continuing on Speed 6, gradually sprinkle in sugar; beat for 4 minutes. Reduce to Stir Speed and add pumpkin. Stop and scrape bowl.

Combine flour, baking powder, cinnamon, nutmeg, and ground ginger. Turn to Stir Speed and gradually add flour mixture to egg mixture, about 1 minute.

Line 9 x 13 x ¾-inch jelly roll pan with waxed paper and grease well. Pour mixture into pan and bake at 375°F for 12 to 13 minutes. Remove from oven and immediately turn onto a towel sprinkled with powdered sugar. Remove waxed paper and roll cake and towel together; place on rack to cool completely.

When cool, unroll cake and spread with *Cream Cheese Filling*. Reroll and sprinkle with powdered sugar.

Yield: Nine 1-inch servings.

Cream Cheese Filling

1 package (8 oz.) cream
cheese, softened
4 teaspoons butter or
margarine
½ teaspoon vanilla
1 cup powdered sugar

Place all ingredients in bowl. Attach bowl and flat beater. Turn to Speed 4 and beat until thoroughly combined, about 2 minutes.

Orange Chiffon Cake

Always light and refreshing.

2¼ cups cake flour

1½ cups sugar

3 teaspoons baking powder

1 teaspoon salt

½ cup vegetable oil

5 egg yolks, at room temperature

3 tablespoons grated orange peel

¾ cup orange juice

8 egg whites, at room temperature

½ teaspoon cream of tartar

Sift flour, sugar, baking powder, and salt into bowl. Make a well in the center and add oil, egg yolks, and orange peel. Attach bowl and flat beater. Turn to Speed 2 and beat 30 seconds. Stop and scrape bowl. Add orange juice. Turn to Speed 6 and beat 1 minute. Remove mixture from bowl and set aside.

Place egg whites and cream of tartar in clean bowl. Attach bowl and wire whip. Turn to Speed 8 and whip until stiff but not dry. Fold flour mixture into egg whites, just until blended.

Pour batter into an ungreased 10-inch tube pan. Bake at 325°F for 55 minutes. Increase oven to 350°F and bake 10 minutes longer. Invert cake to cool.

To remove from pan, gently loosen all edges with a paring knife. Place on serving plate and drizzle *Orange Glaze* over top.

Yield: One 10-inch cake.

Orange Glaze

½ cup orange juice

4-5 tablespoons sugar

Place orange juice and sugar in small saucepan. Bring to a boil over medium heat and stir until slightly thickened. Remove from heat and cool.

Cut angel, chiffon or sponge cakes with a long serrated knife, using a gentle sawing motion; or use a cake breaker.

Chocolate Frosting
Everyone's finger-lickin' favorite.

1 cup butter or
  margarine, at room
  temperature
2 egg yolks, at room
  temperature
4 cups powdered sugar
2 squares (2 oz. each)
  unsweetened
  chocolate, melted

Place butter in bowl. Attach bowl and flat beater. Turn to Speed 4 and beat until creamy, about 1½ minutes. Stop and scrape bowl. On Speed 2, add egg yolks, one at a time, mixing thoroughly after each addition. Stop and scrape bowl.

Turn to Speed 4 and add powdered sugar to butter mixture, 1 cup at a time, beating thoroughly after each addition. Stop and scrape bowl. Turn to Speed 2 and slowly add melted chocolate, about 1½ minutes. Stop and scrape bowl. Turn to Speed 4 and beat for 1 minute.

Yield: 3 cups.

Oatmeal Cake
Moist and spicy oatmeal cake with a chewy crisp topping of coconut and walnuts.

1¼ cups boiling water
1 cup rolled oats
½ cup butter or
  margarine, softened
1 cup brown sugar
1 cup sugar
2 teaspoons vanilla
2 eggs
1½ cups all-purpose flour
1 teaspoon baking soda
¾ teaspoon cinnamon
½ teaspoon salt
¼ teaspoon nutmeg

Combine water and oats in a small bowl; set aside.

Place butter, brown sugar, and sugar in bowl. Attach bowl and flat beater. Turn to Speed 4 and beat 1 minute. Stop and scrape bowl.

Add vanilla. Turn to Speed 4 and add eggs, one at a time, beating 15 seconds after each addition. Stop and scrape bowl. Add oat mixture, flour, soda, cinnamon, salt, and nutmeg. Turn to Speed 4 and beat 30 seconds.

Pour batter into a greased and floured 9 x 9 x 2-inch pan. Bake at 350°F for 50 to 55 minutes. Cool cake in pan. When cool, top with *Broiled Coco-Walnut Topping.*

Yield: One 9-inch cake.

Broiled Coco-Walnut Topping

¾ cup shredded coconut
½ cup chopped walnuts
½ cup brown sugar
¼ cup butter or
  margarine, melted
3 tablespoons heavy
  cream

Combine all ingredients thoroughly. Spread on top of cake. Place under broiler until topping is bubbly. Cool before serving.

Queen Mother's Cake

Rich, moist chocolate cake with ground almonds drizzled
with a chocolate-coffee glaze.

¾ cup butter or
   margarine, softened
¾ cup sugar
 6 eggs, separated
 6 ounces sweet
   chocolate, chopped
   and melted
1¼ cups ground almonds
 ⅛ teaspoon salt

Place butter and sugar in bowl. Attach bowl and flat
beater. Turn to Speed 6 and beat 3 minutes, until fluffy.
Stop and scrape bowl.

Turn to Speed 6 and add egg yolks, one at a time, beating
15 seconds after each addition. Stop and scrape bowl. Turn
to Speed 6 and add chocolate; beat 30 seconds. Continuing
on Speed 6, gradually add almonds, beating just until
blended. Remove mixture from bowl and set aside.

Place egg whites and salt in clean bowl. Attach bowl and
wire whip. Turn to Speed 8 and whip until stiff but not
dry. Carefully fold chocolate mixture into egg whites.

Pour batter into a 9-inch springform pan which has been
lined with waxed paper, greased and floured. Bake at
375°F for 20 minutes. Reduce heat to 350°F and bake
50 to 60 minutes longer. Cake should be moist in center
when removed from oven. Cool in pan 20 minutes, then
invert onto serving platter. Pour *Sweet Chocolate Icing*
over cake. Use spatula to smooth top, but allow icing to
run down sides of cake.

Yield: One 9-inch cake.

Sweet Chocolate Icing

½ cup heavy cream
2 teaspoons instant
   coffee
8 ounces sweet
   chocolate, chopped

Scald cream in small saucepan over medium heat. Add
coffee and chocolate, stirring until chocolate is smooth
and completely melted.

Fluffy KitchenAid Frosting

Easy and reliable; part of the KitchenAid tradition.

½ cup water
1½ tablespoons light
   corn syrup
1½ cups sugar
½ teaspoon cream of
   tartar
½ teaspoon salt
2 egg whites
1½ teaspoons vanilla

Place water, corn syrup, sugar, cream of tartar, and salt in a saucepan. Stir over medium heat until sugar is completely dissolved, forming a syrup.

Place egg whites in bowl. Attach bowl and wire whip. Turn to Speed 10 and whip until egg whites begin to hold shape, about 45 seconds. Continuing on Speed 10, gradually add hot syrup in a thin, steady stream, about 1 to 1½ minutes. Add vanilla and continue whipping about 5 minutes or until frosting loses gloss and stands in stiff peaks. Use immediately.

Yield: 3 cups.

Variations:

Fluffy Chocolate Frosting: Melt 3 squares (1 oz. each) unsweetened chocolate with water, corn syrup, cream of tartar, and salt. Proceed as directed above.

Fluffy Peppermint Frosting: Omit vanilla and add 1 teaspoon peppermint extract and ¼ cup crushed peppermint candy. Proceed as directed above.

Fluffy Amaretto Frosting: Omit vanilla and add 2½ teaspoons Amaretto liqueur. Proceed as directed above.

Fluffy Lemon Frosting: Omit vanilla and add 1 teaspoon lemon extract and 2 teaspoons grated lemon peel. Proceed as directed above.

DESSERTS

The last word

What better way to finish a fine meal than with a bit of something sweet. From a tart Lemon Soufflé, to a rich Chocolate Pecan Pie, there's a recipe that will provide just the right ending to a simple everyday meal or a sumptuous feast. Looking for something light and refreshing? Try the Mango Sherbet or Bavarian Creme. A classic creation? The Paris Brest. An old-time favorite with a tasty new twist? Our Country Pear Pie or the Tart Tartin.

Bavarian Crème

A light vanilla crème meant to be set in a pretty mold
and topped with your favorite sauce.

2 envelopes unflavored
    gelatin
⅓ cup water
6 egg yolks
¾ cup sugar
¼ teaspoon salt
1½ cups milk, scalded
1½ teaspoons vanilla
1½ cups heavy cream

Sprinkle gelatin over water to soften; set aside.

Place egg yolks in bowl. Attach bowl and wire whip.
Turn to Speed 10 and beat 1 minute or until light.

Place egg yolks in double boiler over boiling water. Stir
constantly for 30 seconds. *Slowly* sprinkle in sugar and
salt and continue stirring. *Slowly* add milk while stirring
constantly. Cook and stir mixture 1 minute or until
thickened. Remove from heat.

Dissolve softened gelatin over hot water. Stir gelatin into egg mixture. Cool in refrigerator.

Place cream in clean bowl. Attach bowl and wire whip.
Turn to Speed 8 and whip until almost stiff. Reduce to
Stir Speed and add cooled egg mixture, mixing just until
combined. Pour into an oiled 1-quart mold. Refrigerate
until set. If desired, top with fresh raspberry or pineapple
puree just before serving.

Yield: 6 to 8 servings.

Chocolate Pecan Pie

4 eggs
1 cup sugar
1 cup dark corn syrup
3 squares (1 oz. each)
    unsweetened
    chocolate, melted
2 cups pecan halves
1 unbaked 10-inch
    pastry shell

Place eggs, sugar, and corn syrup in bowl. Attach bowl
and flat beater. Turn to Speed 6 and beat 1 minute. Stop
and scrape bowl.

Turn to Speed 4 and gradually add chocolate; beat
1 minute, until well blended. Reduce to Stir Speed and
quickly add pecans. Pour mixture into pastry shell. Bake
at 350°F for 35 to 45 minutes or until slightly soft in
center.

Yield: One 10-inch pie.

KitchenAid Pie Pastry

2¼ cups all-purpose flour
¾ teaspoon salt
½ cup shortening, well
  chilled
2 tablespoons butter or
  margarine, well
  chilled
5-6 tablespoons water,
  well chilled

Sift flour and salt into bowl. Cut shortening and butter into 4 or 5 pieces and drop into bowl. Attach bowl and flat beater. Turn to Stir Speed and cut shortening into flour until particles are size of small peas, about 30 seconds.

Add water, a tablespoon at a time, until all particles are moistened. Use only enough water to make pastry form a ball. Watch dough closely as overmixing will result in a tough crust.

Chill in refrigerator 15 minutes. Roll to ⅛-inch thickness between pieces of waxed paper. Fold pastry into quarters; ease into pie plate and unfold, pressing firmly against bottom and side. Trim and crimp edges. Fill and bake as desired.

Yield: Two 8 or 9-inch single crusts or one 8 or 9-inch double crust.

For Baked Pastry Shell: Prick sides and bottom with fork. Bake at 450°F for 8 to 10 minutes until light brown. Cool completely before filling.

Pots de Crème au Chocolat

A rich chocolate custard which is very continental—and incredibly easy!

2 cups heavy cream
1 tablespoon sugar
4 squares (1 oz. each)
  sweet chocolate,
  melted
3 egg yolks

Heat cream and sugar in double boiler over boiling water, stirring until sugar is dissolved. Add chocolate, stirring until well blended. Remove from heat and set aside.

Place egg yolks in bowl. Attach bowl and wire whip. Turn to Speed 8 and whip 1 minute. Reduce to Speed 2 and gradually add cream mixture, whipping until well blended.

Fill 6-ounce custard cups or creme pots two-thirds full. Place cups in a 9 x 13 x 2-inch pan and add boiling water 1½ inches in depth. Bake at 325°F for 18 to 20 minutes or until firm. Chill at least 2 hours.

Yield: 6 servings.

158

Mango Sherbet

3 ripe mangoes, peeled,
  seeded and quartered
¾ cup sugar
1 envelope (¼ oz.)
  gelatin
1½ cups boiling water
1 cup milk
2 tablespoons lime
  juice
2 egg whites
¼ cup sugar

Assemble and attach Fruit/Vegetable Strainer. Turn to Speed 4 and strain mangoes. Measure out 1½ cups mango puree and set aside.

Place sugar and gelatin in a bowl. Add boiling water and stir until completely dissolved. Cool to lukewarm. Add mango puree, milk, and lime juice; stir well. Freeze until partially frozen, about 1½ hours.

Place egg whites and sugar in mixer bowl. Attach bowl and wire whip. Turn to Speed 10 and whip until stiff but not dry. Reduce to Stir Speed and quickly add mango mixture, whipping just until blended.

Freeze until firm. Let stand at room temperature a few minutes before serving.

Yield: 1 quart.

Mangoes should be ripened at room temperature until they give slightly when pressed. When ripe, mangoes are orange-yellow in color and have a rosy blush on the side exposed to the sun.

Paris Brest

The grand finale—a classic almond cream puff ring with a rich cream filling.

Ring:
- *1 cup water*
- *½ cup butter or margarine*
- *¼ teaspoon salt*
- *1 cup all-purpose flour*
- *4 eggs*
- *¼ cup slivered almonds*

Heat water, butter, and salt in a 1½-quart saucepan over high heat to a full rolling boil. Reduce heat and quickly stir in flour, mixing vigorously until mixture leaves sides of pan in a ball.

Place mixture in bowl. Attach bowl and flat beater. Turn to Speed 2 and add eggs, one at a time, beating 30 seconds after each addition. Stop and scrape bowl. Turn to Speed 4 and beat 15 seconds.

Using a 7-inch waxed paper circle as a guide, drop batter by heaping tablespoons in 10 mounds to form a ring. Sprinkle with slivered almonds. Bake at 400°F for 10 minutes, then reduce heat to 375°F and bake 30 minutes longer. Cut several slits in side of ring. Let stand 15 minutes in turned off oven with door ajar. Cool completely.

Filling:
- *1 cup milk*
- *3 egg yolks*
- *⅓ cup plus 2 tablespoons sugar*
- *2 tablespoons cornstarch*
- *1½ teaspoons almond extract*
- *1 cup heavy cream*
- *Powdered sugar*

Place milk in a small saucepan and bring to a boil over medium heat. Remove from heat, cover and set aside.

Place egg yolks and ⅓ cup sugar in bowl. Attach bowl and wire whip. Turn to Speed 4 and whip 4 minutes, until mixture becomes thick and light colored. Stop and scrape bowl. Turn to Stir Speed and add cornstarch, mixing just until blended. Add 1 teaspoon almond extract to milk. Turn to Speed 2 and gradually add milk to egg mixture, about 30 seconds. Whip 30 seconds longer.

Return mixture to saucepan and bring to a boil over medium heat. Boil 1 minute, stirring constantly. Remove from heat and cool completely. When cool, place egg yolk mixture in bowl. Attach bowl and wire whip. Turn to Speed 4 and whip 1 minute, until fluffy. Remove from bowl and set aside.

Place cream and remaining almond extract in clean bowl. Attach bowl and wire whip. Turn to Speed 8 and whip until cream begins to thicken. Continuing on Speed 8, gradually add remaining sugar, whipping until stiff. Reduce to Stir Speed and add egg yolk mixture, whipping just until blended.

Slice ring in half crosswise to form a top and bottom. Spoon filling into bottom of ring. Place top of ring on filling and dust with powdered sugar. Chill before serving.

Yield: 10 servings.

Lemon Soufflé
Delicate and tangy, this will delight the eye as well as the palate.

2 tablespoons butter or
  margarine
⅓ cup plus 3 tablespoons
  sugar
2 tablespoons grated
  fresh lemon peel
3 tablespoons all-
  purpose flour
¾ cup milk
⅓ cup fresh lemon juice
5 eggs, separated

Grease a 1½-quart soufflé dish with 1 tablespoon butter. Combine 3 tablespoons sugar and 1 tablespoon grated lemon peel. Sprinkle soufflé dish with mixture; set aside.

Melt remaining butter in saucepan over medium heat. Add flour and blend well; cook 1 minute. Gradually add milk, stirring until smooth. Add sugar and bring to a boil, stirring constantly for 30 seconds. Place mixture in bowl. Turn to Speed 4 and beat 1 minute. Stop and scrape bowl. Turn to Speed 6 and add egg yolks, one at a time, beating 15 seconds after each addition. Remove from bowl and set aside.

Place egg whites in clean bowl. Attach bowl and wire whip. Turn to Speed 8 and whip until stiff but not dry. Gently fold egg yolk mixture into egg whites. Pour into soufflé dish. Run a knife around soufflé inserted 1½ inches deep and 1 inch from the edge.

Place soufflé dish in a 9 x 13 x 2-inch pan and add boiling water 1 inch in depth. Bake at 350°F for 25 to 30 minutes. Serve immediately.

Yield: 6 to 8 servings.

Almond Dacquoise

Three layers of meringue frosted with rich chocolate buttercream; sinfully rich.

6 ounces blanched
  almonds, ground
1 cup powdered sugar
1½ tablespoons
  cornstarch
6 egg whites
⅛ teaspoon salt
¼ teaspoon cream of
  tartar
3 tablespoons sugar
1¼ teaspoons vanilla
¼ teaspoon almond
  extract

Combine almonds, powdered sugar, and cornstarch; set aside.

Place egg whites in bowl. Attach bowl and wire whip. Turn to Speed 6 and whip until foamy. Add salt and cream of tartar and continue whipping until soft peaks form. Sprinkle in sugar, vanilla, and almond extract, beating until stiff peaks form. Reduce to Stir Speed and quickly add almond mixture, mixing just until blended.

Force mixture through pastry bag fitted with wide tube (½-inch) onto greased and floured baking sheets to form three 8-inch circles. Bake at 250°F for 35 to 45 minutes. Remove from baking sheets and cool on aluminum foil. Fill and frost with *Chocolate Buttercream Filling*.

Yield: One 8-inch cake.

Chocolate Buttercream Filling

2 egg yolks
1 cup powdered sugar
2 squares (1 oz. each)
  semi-sweet chocolate,
  melted
¾ cup butter or
  margarine, softened
½ teaspoon vanilla

Place egg yolks in bowl. Attach bowl and wire whip. Turn to Speed 6 and whip 2 minutes. Stop and scrape bowl.

Turn to Speed 4 and gradually add powdered sugar, chocolate, butter, and vanilla; continue beating 5 minutes or until fluffy.

Wafer Torte

Layers of Amaretto-soaked chocolate wafers and rich
chocolate mousse topped with fresh whipped cream.

7 squares (1 oz. each) semi-sweet chocolate 6 eggs, separated 2 teaspoons vanilla 1 package (8 oz.) chocolate wafer cookies ⅓ cup Amaretto liqueur ½ cup heavy cream	Melt chocolate in double boiler over boiling water. Add egg yolks and vanilla; beat well. Remove from heat and set aside. Place egg whites in bowl. Attach bowl and wire whip. Turn to Speed 8 and whip until stiff but not dry. Reduce to Stir Speed and quickly add chocolate mixture, mixing just until combined. Arrange half of wafers in the bottom of a 9-inch springform pan. Brush wafers with half of Amaretto and top with half of chocolate mixture. Repeat with remaining ingredients. Refrigerate until set, about 5 hours. When ready to serve, unmold from pan and place on serving plate. Place cream in bowl. Attach bowl and wire whip. Turn to Speed 10 and whip cream until stiff. Serve with torte. *Yield:* One 9-inch torte.

Lemon Cheese Pie

Crust: 1½ cups graham cracker crumbs ¼ cup butter or margarine, melted ¼ cup brown sugar 1 teaspoon cinnamon	Place all ingredients in bowl. Attach bowl and flat beater. Turn to Speed 2 and mix 30 seconds. Press mixture into a 9-inch pie plate. Bake at 350°F for 3 minutes. Cool on wire rack.
Filling: 4 packages (3 oz. each) cream cheese, softened 2 eggs ½ cup sugar 2 teaspoons grated lemon peel ¼ cup lemon juice	Place all ingredients in bowl. Attach bowl and wire whip. Turn to Speed 4 and whip 30 seconds. Stop and scrape bowl. Turn to Speed 4 and whip 15 seconds more. Pour into crust and bake at 350°F for 30 to 35 minutes. *Yield:* One 9-inch pie.

Country Pear Pie

¾ cup brown sugar
3 tablespoons all-
   purpose flour
⅛ teaspoon salt
   Dash ground cloves
   Dash nutmeg
⅓ cup heavy cream
8-10 medium pears (about
   2½ pounds) pared,
   cored and thinly sliced
2 tablespoons lemon
   juice
2 tablespoons butter or
   margarine
   KitchenAid pie pastry
   for double crust
   9-inch pie

In a small bowl, combine brown sugar, flour, salt, cloves, and nutmeg. Stir in cream. In another bowl, sprinkle lemon juice over pears. Add brown sugar and cream mixture and mix well. Set aside.

Divide pastry in half. Roll to ⅛-inch thickness and line a 9-inch pie plate. Fill with pear mixture and dot with butter. Roll out remaining pastry and cut into ½-inch strips. Weave strips into a lattice on top of pears. Seal and crimp edges. Bake at 400°F for 35 to 40 minutes.

Yield: One 9-inch pie.

Raspberry Crème

For raspberry lovers everywhere!

1½ tablespoons gelatin
¼ cup cold water
2 packages (12 oz. each)
   frozen raspberries,
   thawed
2 cups heavy cream
½ cup sugar
   Dash salt
1½ tablespoons lemon
   juice

Sprinkle gelatin over cold water in a small saucepan to soften.

Assemble and attach Fruit/Vegetable Strainer. Turn to Speed 4 and strain raspberries into bowl. Add 1 cup cream, sugar, and salt. Attach bowl and wire whip. Turn to Stir Speed and mix until well blended.

Place gelatin over low heat to dissolve. Add lemon juice. Turn to Stir Speed and gradually add gelatin mixture to raspberry mixture and beat 1 minute, until well blended. Remove from bowl and set aside.

Place remaining cream in clean bowl. Attach bowl and wire whip. Turn to Speed 8 and whip until stiff. Reduce to Stir Speed and add raspberry mixture, mixing just until blended. Freeze mixture until partially set, stirring occasionally during freezing. Serve in long-stemmed glasses.

Yield: 6 to 8 servings.

Orange Angel Pie

A sweet meringue shell with a tart orange filling laden with mounds of whipped cream.

4 egg whites
1½ teaspoons vanilla
1 cup plus 2 teaspoons powdered sugar
¾ cup sugar
2½ tablespoons cornstarch
⅛ teaspoon salt
¾ cup orange juice
2 tablespoons grated fresh orange peel
2 tablespoons butter or margarine
1 cup heavy cream

Place egg whites in bowl. Attach bowl and wire whip. Turn to Speed 8 and whip until foamy. Continuing on Speed 8, add 1 teaspoon vanilla and gradually add powdered sugar, beating until stiff but not dry. Spread mixture on bottom and sides of a greased 9-inch glass pie plate. Bake at 225°F for 1 hour 15 minutes. Turn oven off and allow crust to cool with oven door ajar.

Combine sugar, cornstarch, salt, and orange juice in small saucepan over medium heat. Cook and stir until well blended, then boil 1 minute. Remove mixture from heat and add orange peel and butter; blend well. Refrigerate mixture 15 minutes, then pour into shell and refrigerate 1 to 2 hours.

Place remaining vanilla, sugar, and cream in bowl. Attach bowl and wire whip. Turn to Speed 8 and whip until stiff. Spread whipped cream on pie and serve immediately.

Yield: One 9-inch pie.

Key Lime Pie

Choose only the freshest limes for this Southern favorite.

2 cups sugar
¼ cup plus 2 tablespoons cornstarch
¼ teaspoon salt
½ cup fresh lime juice
½ cup cold water
3 eggs, separated
2 tablespoons butter or margarine
1½ cups boiling water
1 teaspoon grated fresh lime peel
Green food coloring (if desired)
¼ teaspoon cream of tartar
1 baked KitchenAid 9-inch pastry shell

Filling: Combine 1½ cups sugar, cornstarch, and salt in a 2-quart saucepan. Add lime juice, water, and egg yolks; blend well. Add butter and gradually add boiling water. Bring mixture to a boil over medium heat and cook 3 minutes, stirring constantly. Stir in lime peel and green food coloring. Remove from heat and cool 20 minutes.

Meringue: Place egg whites in bowl. Attach bowl and wire whip. Turn to Speed 8 and whip until frothy. Add cream of tartar and whip until soft peaks form. Continuing on Speed 8, gradually add remaining sugar, beating until stiff peaks form.

Pour cooled filling into pie shell. Lightly pile meringue on filling and spread to edges. Bake at 350°F for 15 minutes, or until lightly browned. Cool completely before serving.

Yield: One 9-inch pie.

Tart Tartin

An upside-down apple tart.

1¼ cups butter or margarine
⅓ cup sugar
¼ cup brown sugar
½ cup fresh bread crumbs
6 tart cooking apples, peeled, cored and thinly sliced
1 tablespoon grated lemon peel
¼ cup lemon juice
1 tablespoon Triple Sec liqueur
KitchenAid pie pastry for 9-inch single crust pie

Place 1 cup butter, sugar, brown sugar, and bread crumbs in bowl. Attach bowl and flat beater. Turn to Speed 4 and mix 30 seconds, until blended. Pat mixture on bottom and up sides of a 10-inch pie plate.

Place apples in a large bowl. Sprinkle lemon peel, lemon juice, and Triple Sec over apples and toss gently to mix. Arrange apple mixture in pie plate. Melt remaining ¼ cup butter and pour over apple mixture.

Roll out pastry dough to fit top of pie plate. Seal edges and cut slits for steam to escape. Place on a baking sheet and bake at 400°F for 45 to 50 minutes. Cool in plate 15 minutes, then invert onto serving platter. Serve warm.

Yield: One 10-inch tart.

Zuccotto

An Italian specialty of fresh strawberries and whipped cream
molded in slices of pound cake sprinkled with liqueur.

*1 package (10¾ oz.)
pound cake, cut into
½-inch slices*
*4 tablespoons Amaretto
liqueur*
1½ cups heavy cream
½ cup sugar
1 teaspoon vanilla
*1 cup fresh strawberries,
mashed*

Line a 1½-quart bowl with cheesecloth. Cut pound cake slices in half diagonally to form triangles. Line bowl with ⅔ of cake triangles. Sprinkle with Amaretto and set aside.

Place 1 cup cream, ¼ cup sugar, and vanilla in bowl. Attach bowl and wire whip. Turn to Speed 8 and whip until stiff. Spoon into cake-lined bowl.

Place remaining cream and sugar in bowl. Attach bowl and wire whip. Turn to Speed 10 and whip until stiff. Reduce to Stir Speed and quickly add strawberries, whipping just until blended. Spread strawberry mixture on top of whipped cream. Arrange remaining cake slices on top of strawberry mixture. Fold ends of cheesecloth over cake and cover tightly with plastic wrap. Freeze 4 to 5 hours.

To serve, dip bowl in hot water a few seconds, then invert onto a platter. Remove cheesecloth and cut into wedges.

Yield: 6 to 8 servings.

Chocolate Peanut Torte

¾ cup butter or
   margarine, softened
¾ cup sugar
 6 ounces almond paste
 5 eggs
⅔ cup graham cracker
   crumbs
¾ cup all-purpose flour
¾ teaspoon baking
   powder
1⅓ cups ground peanuts

Place butter, sugar, and almond paste in bowl. Attach bowl and flat beater. Turn to Speed 4 and beat 1 minute. Continuing on Speed 4, add eggs, one at a time, beating 15 seconds after each addition. Stop and scrape bowl.

Turn to Speed 2 and gradually add graham cracker crumbs, flour, and baking powder; beat 1 minute more. Reduce to Stir Speed and quickly add peanuts, mixing just until blended.

Pour batter into a 9-inch springform pan which has been lined with waxed paper and greased. Bake at 350°F for 50 to 55 minutes. Remove from pan and cool on wire rack.

When cool, slice cake in thirds to form three layers. Frost with *Chocolate Peanut Frosting*.

Yield: One 9-inch torte.

Chocolate Peanut Frosting

½ cup butter or
   margarine, softened
½ cup powdered sugar
 2 ounces almond paste
1⅓ cups creamy peanut
   butter
 4 squares (1 oz. each)
   semi-sweet chocolate,
   melted

Place butter, powdered sugar, and almond paste in bowl. Attach bowl and flat beater. Turn to Speed 4 and beat 2 minutes. Stop and scrape bowl.

Add peanut butter and chocolate. Turn to Speed 6 and beat 2 minutes, until fluffy.

ATTACHMENTS & ACCESSORIES

Cooking with
KitchenAid
Attachments and
Accessories

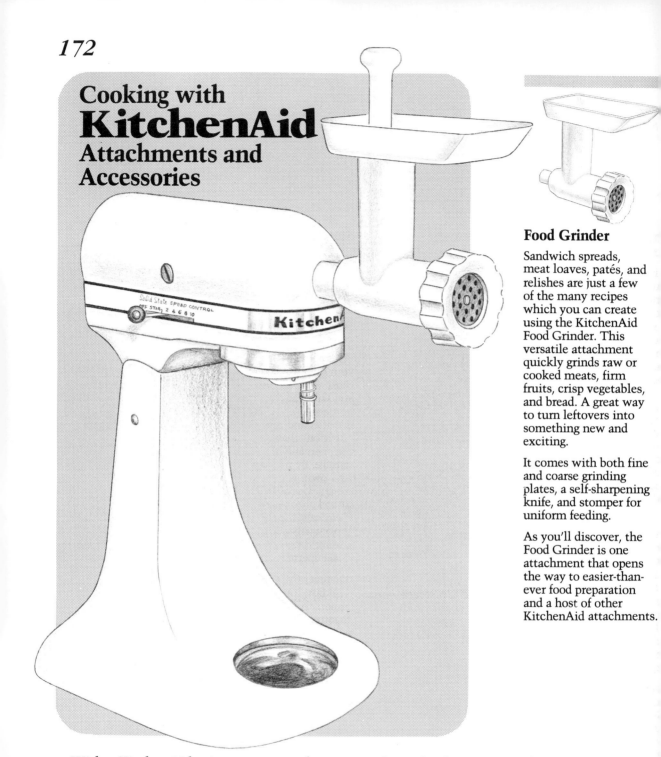

Food Grinder

Sandwich spreads, meat loaves, patés, and relishes are just a few of the many recipes which you can create using the KitchenAid Food Grinder. This versatile attachment quickly grinds raw or cooked meats, firm fruits, crisp vegetables, and bread. A great way to turn leftovers into something new and exciting.

It comes with both fine and coarse grinding plates, a self-sharpening knife, and stomper for uniform feeding.

As you'll discover, the Food Grinder is one attachment that opens the way to easier-than-ever food preparation and a host of other KitchenAid attachments.

With a KitchenAid mixer, you can plan on spending a lot less time in the kitchen. Because when it comes to food preparation, KitchenAid mixers are designed to do a lot more than mixing, kneading and whipping.

Today's models, the K45SS and the K5SS, as well as many older KitchenAid models, are powered to operate a wide variety of work and timesaving optional attachments and accessories. Every one comes with easy-to-follow instructions.

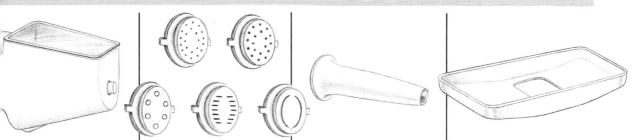

ruit/Vegetable rainer

ith the KitchenAid uit/Vegetable rainer, you can ocess large quantities garden fresh fruits d vegetables in less ne than you might nagine. It purees, ices, and strains soft ods for use in asoned sauces, eamy soups, side shes, fruit fillings, d jams. It's also an onomical way for other to prepare baby ods free from additives, d great for people soft food diets.

ne Fruit/Vegetable rainer uses the tchenAid Food rinder housing fitted th a special worm sembly and strainer ne to separate food lp from seeds, peelings, d core, doing away with e need for you to epare them by hand.

you already own a od Grinder, Model -A, you can convert nto this great time- ving attachment nply by purchasing a of Fruit/Vegetable rainer Parts. Other- se, just ask for this o-in-one attachment name...the KitchenAid uit/Vegetable Strainer d Food Grinder.

Pasta Maker

Now you, too, can experience the special flavor and texture of homemade pasta as often as you like using the KitchenAid Pasta Maker attachment. Packed with five plates, it extrudes pasta dough into thick and thin spaghetti, flat noodles, macaroni, and lasagna.

Create a variety of mouth-watering dishes using fresh pasta in soups, salads, casseroles, or smothered in your favorite sauce.

If you already own a Food Grinder attach- ment, Model FG-A, you can begin to make homemade pasta simply by purchasing a set of pasta plates. In no time at all, you'll be on your way to becoming a pasta pro!

Sausage Stuffer

If the thought of mak- ing homemade sausage sounds interesting, it is. And quite simple, too, when you use the KitchenAid Sausage Stuffer.

Whether you create your own recipes or use those we have provided, you will also discover that homemade sausage is tastier and more nutritious than commercially-made sausage. By making your own, you control the amount of salt and fat and eliminate the chemicals and fillers customarily added to sausage found at your local supermarket.

Whatever the fare... breakfast, lunch, or dinner...this often forgotten art is sure to be as satisfying as it is delectable.

Food Tray

If you often process large quantities of fruits, vegetables, and meats, the KitchenAid Food Tray is one accessory you'll want to own. Intended for use with the Food Grinder and the Fruit/ Vegetable Strainer, this accessory increases the capacity of the hopper, helping to reduce the number of times you need to fill it with food. Easy to attach as it glides securely into place over the hopper.

Attachments and Accessories

Rotor Slicer/Shredder

The secret of the KitchenAid Rotor Slicer/Shredder is its openmouth, split-hopper design. With this popular KitchenAid attachment, you can slice and shred a colorful assortment of firm fruits and vegetables as quickly as you can fill the hopper. Slice cucumbers, carrots, cabbage, potatoes, or other foods for your favorite salads, slaws, and relishes. Or shred firm cheese, nuts, chocolate, even coconut for appetizers, main dishes, and desserts. Process an entire hopper full or just a single item.

Packed with four chrome-plated cones for thick and thin slicing and coarse and fine shredding, the Rotor Slicer/Shredder can help you work better and faster.

Grain Mill

Share in the good taste and nutritious benefit of whole grain breads, muffins, and other baked goods by milling your own flour in the KitchenAid Grain Mill. Wheat, rye, oats, rice, corn, and many other low moisture, non-oily grains can all be ground. Made of heavy cast metal, it has hardened steel burrs which can be adjusted to provide a range of grind settings from fine flour to cracked grain.

With a little bit of creativity and experience, you will discover how simple it is to add some whole grain goodness to your family's favorite recipes.

Pouring Shield

Whether you use your mixer everyday or just now and then, the Pouring Shield is one accessory you won't want to do without. Designed to sit neatly on the rim of the mixer bowl, it allows you to easily add ingredients and minimizes any splashing during operation. Specially sized for each mixer model.

Can Opener

The KitchenAid Can Opener handles all your can opening needs with the added convenience of saving on counter space. Opens cans of any shape and size, up to two pounds. Safe and simple to use. Magnet picks up the lid and the can is held securely in place until released.

Citrus Juicer

Enjoy the flavor of fresh squeezed juice each and every day without the bother of doing it by hand. Easy to assemble and attach, the Citrus Juicer juices oranges, grapefruits, lemons, and limes. Simply hold the fruit to the reamer, turn your mixer on, and fresh juice is ready for drinks and recipes. A detachable strainer conveniently separates seeds and pulp from juice.

Water Jacket

The KitchenAid Water Jacket helps maintain the temperature of ingredients during preparation. Made of heavy tin dipped steel, it is designed to hang below the bowl. Fill it with ice to whip cream or special frostings; or with hot water to whip potatoes, turnips, and other vegetables, or those desserts which need warm water to assure good volume. For K5 mixer models only.

Common Cooking Measurements, Equivalents and Substitutions

Apples	1 lb. (3-4 medium)	3 cups pared, sliced
Baking Powder	1 teaspoon	¼ teaspoon baking soda plus ⅝ teaspoon cream of tartar
		¼ teaspoon baking soda plus ½ cup buttermilk or yogurt
Bananas	1 lb.	1⅓ cups, mashed
Bread Crumbs, dry	¼ cup	1 slice bread
fresh	½ cup	1 slice bread
Broth, chicken or beef	1 cup	1 bouillon cube or 1 teaspoon powdered broth or stock base dissolved in 1 cup boiling water
Butter or Margarine 1 stick	4 oz.	8 tablespoons or ½ cup
4 sticks	1 lb.	2 cups
Cheese, American or Cheddar	¼ lb	1 cup shredded
cottage	1 lb.	2 cups
cream	3 oz.	6 tablespoons
	8 oz.	1 cup (16 tablespoons)
Chocolate, unsweetened	1 sq. (1 oz.)	3 tablespoons cocoa plus 1 tablespoon butter or vegetable oil
Coconut, flaked	3½ oz.	1⅓ cups
Cream, heavy or whipping	½ pint (1 cup)	2 to 2½ cups whipped
Egg Whites, large	8-10 whites	1 cup
Egg Yolks, large	12-14 yolks	1 cup
Flour, all-purpose	1 lb.	about 3½ cups
cake	1 lb.	about 4 cups
Gelatin, unflavored	¼ oz. envelope	1 tablespoon
Lemon	1 medium	2-3 tablespoons juice
		1½-2 teaspoons grated peel
	1 teaspoon grated peel	½ teaspoon lemon extract
Lime	1 medium	2 tablespoons juice
Milk, whole	1 cup	½ cup evaporated plus ½ cup water
		1 cup reconstituted nonfat dry milk plus 2½ teaspoons butter or margarine

Nuts, shelled	¼ lb	1 cup chopped
(peanuts, pecans, walnuts)		
Onion	1 medium	½-¾ cup, chopped
Orange	1 medium	⅓-½ cup juice
		2-3 tablespoons grated peel
Potatoes	1 lb	3 medium
Raisins, seedless	1 lb	2¾ cups
Rice, regular	1 cup uncooked	about 3 cups cooked
Sugar,		
granulated	1 lb	2-2¼ cups
brown	1 lb	2¼ cups firmly packed
confectioners' or		
powdered	1 lb	3½-4 cups
Tomatoes	1 lb	3 medium
		2 cups chopped
Yogurt	1 cup	1 cup buttermilk

dash	2 to 3 drops, or less than ⅛ teaspoon	½ pint (liquid)	1 cup
1 tablespoon	3 teaspoons	1 pint	2 cups
¼ cup	4 tablespoons	1 quart	4 cups
⅓ cup	5⅓ tablespoons	1 gallon	4 quarts
½ cup	8 tablespoons	1 peck (dry)	8 quarts
¾ cup	12 tablespoons	1 bushel	4 pecks
1 cup	16 tablespoons	1 pound	16 ounces

INDEX

Customer Relations Department
KitchenAid Division, Hobart Corporation
Troy, Ohio 45374

Book design by Vincent J. Ciancio